So, You Think
You Know Rhode Island?

People, Places, Folklore, Trivia
and Treasures

By Bobby Oliveira

Omni Publishing Co.
2023

Published by Omni Publishing Co.
www.omni-pub.com

Cover Design: Dave Derby
www.DerbyCreative.com

Library of Congress cataloging in publication data
Oliveira, Bobby

So, You Think You Know Rhode Island?
People, Places, Folklore, Trivia and Treasures

ISBN: 978-1-928758-09-9

Author Information

Bobby Oliveira is the Treasurer of the Quahogs United PAC and the creator of the Quahogs United Blog. He has more than 40 years of campaign experience and more than 35 years of sales experience, including from 2007-2011 when he was Sales Director at the Newport Bay Club until he sold out the inventory. He also has 30 years of writing experience going back to his time as a newsman at WHTB Radio and moving on to become the head speechwriter to future State Senator and Democratic Chair Rep. Joan Menard.

Mr. Oliveira has campaigned in 38 states. Most of this experience was garnered when he worked on Presidential campaigns in 1988 and 1992. He is a veteran of multiple New Hampshire Presidential Primaries. Along the way, he has also served on teams that have been successful lobbying for laws and ordinances in 4 states. Due to that experience, he is a go to for various forms of public records requests including APRAs, FOILs, and FOIAs. When not doing that, he is often tasked to write radio commercials. He has done that for candidates at the municipal, county, state, and Federal levels.

Most memorable of those experiences happened back in the mid-nineties. Dr. Irving Fradkin, of Dollars for Scholars fame, asked Bobby to change the city of Fall River's motto from "We'll try" to "Scholarship City." Thanks to Bobby's leadership, the City of Fall River's City Council voted in the affirmative for the change.

His sales career started in real estate rentals. From that, he had a 10 year career in floorcovering. Back in 1999, he secured the contract for the floorcovering in the Pfizer labs in Groton, Connecticut. In 2000, he was recruited by a timeshare firm and went on to have a 16 year career in timeshares and vacation clubs. He still sells ads for his blog from time to time. He has sold those products in 5 states.

While he has created political change and profit all over the country, he is most proud of his over 20 years clean and sober. He regularly works with newcomers so they can find the same peace he has. While he has a number of mental illnesses, he is able to manage 24 hours at a time. As a result, he has been asked to speak on addiction issues in the same number of states he has campaigned in.

As this is being written, Bobby has recruited a lawyer to represent Rhode Island's homeless camped out at the State House against an illegal eviction order the Governor brought forward. So far the combination of legal resources Bobby has brought together has beaten the Governor twice in court. Bobby hopes this will draw attention to the real services the homeless need, especially regarding addiction and mental illness issues.

Introduction

When the first visitors from Europe arrived in what would become the Colony of Rhode Island and Providence Plantations, they discovered the Wampanoag, Narragansett, and Niantic Tribes. Sadly, many members of the Tribes would be killed by disease and warfare with other tribes. Even the Narragansett language almost disappeared entirely.

In 1636, the Narragansetts would grant land at the tip of Narragansett Bay to Roger Williams who would settle there. In return, he would try to preserve the Narragansett Language in his work A Key to the Languages of America.

Religious and political dissidents would confer with Roger Williams, Anne Hutchinson, and, William Coddington, whose grave was the location for my 5th step, and John Clarke took part in the Portsmouth Compact and settled the area of Portsmouth on what is now Aquidneck Island. Because some people just could not get along, Newport became its own settlement to the South. At one point, Newport almost became its own state.

Rhode Island seemed to attract those who would get into conflict. Samuel Gorton purchased lands at the Shawomet and immediately got into a tussle with the Plymouth Bay Colony. Thankfully Gorton was friends with the Earl of Warwick. The King of England granted a separate charter in 1648, which Mr. Gorton named Warwick after his buddy. A couple of years earlier in 1644, Providence, Portsmouth, and Newport united as the Colony of Rhode Island and Providence Plantations. Finally all 4 factions were united by the Charter of 1663. Observers immediately coined the new Colony "Rogue's Island. They would never let early Rhode Islanders forget who if you got banished from the Massachusetts Bay Colony, there was a place that would welcome you.

Rhode Island is now home to just over 1 million people. Rhode Island is the 17th richest state in the country and the 9th most expensive to afford a home in. That's what happens when so much of the state's property is so close to the water. For 5 decades, Rhode Island has been a solidly Democratic state. The last time a Republican won at the statewide or Congressional level was a decade ago.

Stuffed quahogs are the favorite food in Rhode Island. The mollusks are often combined with a breaded stuffing that is often mixed with Chourico in Portuguese and Azorean households. Most Rhode Island kids are introduced to fishing and digging for clams and quahogs at a very early age.

"Like a bunch of Renegade Pilgrims

Who are thrown out of Plymouth Colony

We are Rhode Island bound.

Or like a group of college freshmen

Who were rejected by Harvard and forced to

go to Brown

We're Rhode Island Bound."

-The Rhode to Rhode Island - Family Guy

Table of Contents

Rhode Island has 400 miles of New England coastline, making it a perfect destination for beach lovers.

Question: What is the name of this historic lighthouse?
Answer on page 161

All About East Bay

The Narragansett Bay divides Southern Rhode Island into 3 parts. The West Bay, Aquidneck Island and Jamestown, and the East Bay are all bordered by the Narragansett Bay. Bristol, Warren, Barrington, Tiverton, Little Compton make up the East Bay Region.

For many environmentalists, the biggest feature of the East Bay is the East Bay Bike Path. The Bike Path actually covers 14.3 miles running from Bristol all the way to Providence. The Bike Path was inducted into the Rail Trail Hall of Fame in 2009. On any given day during any given Bike Path trip, you will observe nature in action.

When you get done with the Bike Path, you can head over to Tiverton. Yes, you will observe nature doing amazing things along the coast. The town I grew up in is strikingly beautiful. When you have had enough beauty to wipe away any bad thoughts or remembrances, you can make a trip over to Fort Barton.

The Fort Barton Site, which also has a nature trail, was a British defensive fort constructed in 1777. Its job at the time was to oversee the Ferry Crossing between Tiverton and Aquidneck Island. When the Colonies took it over, it was named for Lt. Col. William Barton who had conducted a midnight raid on the British Headquarters in Portsmouth. When I was a kid I went to the Fort Barton School. It's still there, and I attended the yearly reenactment.

The East Bay employs close to 20,000 workers in industries such as manufacturing, high tech, and healthcare. If you are not in one of these industries there are two other things you might be doing. Many people who work at the Naval Undersea Warfare Center (NUWC) live in the East Bay. They are engineers mostly just like my dad was.

The other "secret business" of the East Bay is gateway tourism. Many folks want to visit both Newport and Providence without the hassles or the traffic. While still somewhat on the expensive side, the prices in the East Bay thanks to different vacation services are definitely more moderate. Not only can you sneak off to Newport or Providence, but the Cape even by the back roads is only 90 minutes away.

Now you could drive down to Little Compton to run into actress Arden Myrin or head over to Barrington hoping to run into NASA Scientist Carolyn Huntoon. However, if you're like most folks, you'll just wait for the annual 4th of July Parade in Bristol.

The Military, Civic, and Firemen's Parade was founded in 1785. It is the oldest Independence Day celebration in the United States. Before the pandemic, it was not uncommon for 50,000 people to attend the parade. Usually in the 50,000 were a number of celebrities.

The East Bay is worth visiting for the beauty alone. It can be said that the region captures the early American story. On the same day, you can have a picnic breakfast in Bristol's Colt State Park, spend the early afternoon taking a ferry and exploring Prudence Island, and then just before dinner, visit the Wilbor House in Little Compton and discover all kinds of things you didn't know. On the way to the Wilbor House, there are plenty of places to purchase stuffed quahogs, fried clams, or even fresh seafood that just arrived by boat.

There are about 76,000 people living in the East Bay. The average home price is in the $516,000 neighborhood. Most married couples in the region bring in around $108,000 combined. The average age is about 41. Because the East Bay is laid out the way it is, it creates some interesting circumstances leading to higher property values. For instance, while you're in Barrington, you're never more than 2 miles from salt water. Yes, having an interest in water activities, even when it gets a little cold, is a major attraction. There are 12 beaches to choose from.

It's not only the water that makes it different. The East Bay communities tend to have a slightly higher elevation. That in turn causes the sandstone and rock to not erode as quickly as in other places. Many children have discovered this while on vacation and many buckets of rocks end up in cars on the way back home.

People of Significance – East Bay

Robert Gray (May 10, 1755 - July 1806) was the first American Merchant Sea Captain to circumnavigate the globe. His trips to the Northern Pacific Coast pioneered the maritime fur trade. On his second trip, he visited and named the Columbia River.

He started out as just a guy serving in the Continental Navy during the Revolution. After his two Pacific trips he set up shop on the Atlantic. He had planned to make one more Pacific voyage but the French got in the way and captured his boat.

That wouldn't stop him however. He and his wife Martha (Atkins) had 5 kids. He wanted to show them that working meant something. Unfortunately, that need to work hard caused him to catch Yellow Fever while at sea and died out on the Atlantic.

James DeWolf (March 18, 1764 - December 21, 1837) came from a big family. He had 8 brothers and sisters. Something in that experience drove him to desire wealth beyond belief. He too started life as a sailor. He would get captured by the British twice.

However, none of that deterred him from reaching one goal after another. It should be noted that he felt his goals were above the law. Even though slave trading was outlawed in the state of Rhode Island in 1787, Mr. James D'Wolf, as he liked to write, couldn't invest enough money in bringing slaves out of West Africa.

9

In 1791, everything almost fell apart. He was indicted by a grand jury in Newport for killing a female slave two years earlier. No one really doubted the facts. The slave had smallpox. At the time, if a slave got smallpox, they were lowered overboard to avoid the rest of the crew from getting it. After he got indicted he ran off to the West Indies. AS it turned out, the Prosecutor did not decide to pursue the case.

Meanwhile, some tallies have him bringing over 10,000 slaves to the United States whether it was legal or not.

Slaves weren't his only interests. He also invested in sugar and coffee. He had to find something else to entertain him so in 1798 he turned to politics and ran for the Rhode Island House of Representatives. He would serve for 23 of the next 39 years.

The height of his career happened right after he was Speaker from 1819 - 1821. He was selected to be one of Rhode Island's Senators at the Federal level. However, the 20th Amendment, forcing the election of US Senators by the people, became the handwriting on the wall. He would resign in 1825 not even completing a term.

When he died while living in New York City, by all estimations he was a millionaire. Many thought he was the second richest man in the United States. There's no record of how much money each of the 12 kids got. At least his wife, Nancy, got a boat named after her.

Russell Warren (1783-1860) is someone whose folks everybody loves and most folks have no idea they're staring at something he designed. Think of your favorite local building built anywhere between 1800 and 1860. There's a good chance that if he wasn't the chief architect, he was at least on the team. Those buildings would include the Westminster Arcade in Providence, the Levi Gale House at 89 Touro Street in Newport, the original New Bedford City Hall which is now a free public library. Go online and look up 89 Touro Street. Your immediate reaction will be, "I've been there . . . that's who did that . . . that's who owns it . . . I never would have thought . . ."

Mr. Warren was born in Tiverton. As a teenager he moved to Bristol and began to design and build homes. He had many partners throughout his career. In 1823, he moved to Georgetown, South Carolina where he spent most of his time as a contractor.

Something else happened while he was in South Carolina. He became a Greek architectural style enthusiast. He never went to Greece but someone turned him on to the Greek flavor. When he returned in 1826, it became his signature. Most famously, he designed 3 houses in Bristol on Hope Street right next to each other using the Greek building philosophy.

Sarah Helen Whitman (January 19, 1803 - June 27, 1878) was far ahead of her time in so many ways. Her dad was a Providence merchant. He was also "kinda busy." So busy that she started life in a Quaker school on Long Island.

Later she returned to Providence, where she started to study French, German, and Italian. She was especially interested in poetry. She figured why just read when she can write?

She got married in 1828. Unfortunately, Ms. Whitman's husband died in 1833. She was already published in women's magazines. People are noticing that the death has had an effect on her and her writing has a religious tilt.

Prior to 1848, she ends up meeting someone whose writing she has loved for a while. She has a literary salon in her home and everybody from Emerson to Hale to Hay would come and visit. There were always rumors about her interest in "brief romantic relationships. We know she has one of these with Edgar Alan Poe.

In 1848, they had a fling. He died a year later. Much like the death of her husband, this death has a great effect on her writing. Many claim it was his death that inspired her to become a leader in the early Spiritualism movement. She is on this list not because you can visit her vibes at 88 Benefit Street in Providence but because she would tell friends most of her inspiration came from the East Bay. It's almost as if the wind and the waves were as much as inspiration in her looking for answers as the death of her romantic partner was.

Thomas Bicknell (September 6, 1834 - October 6, 1925) was a journeyman far ahead of his time. Born in Rhode Island, went off to college in Vermont and at Amherst. He started his career as a principal in Illinois.

He came back to Rehoboth. Decided to attend Brown. After college, he was a principal at multiple schools in Bristol. While all that was happening, he decided he hated slavery. He also hated discrimination against women. He was an early member of the Free Kansas movement. He decided he needs to be "on the ground." Some bandits on the Missouri thought he'd do better as a hostage. Thanks to some sharpshooters, he was free to return to Rhode Island again.

When he returns, he will help Tiverton elect the first all-female School Board. After that, he managed to become President of the American Institute of Instruction and the National Educational Association. That wasn't enough to keep him busy so he became President of the New England Publishing Company.

Folks were starting to notice his work. He was a member of the U.S. Postal Congress in 1878 where he was part of the U.S. Postal Code's development. Somehow he served as President of 30 different organizations at one time or another.

That's not the coolest story about him though. When he turned 80, he thought the end was near. Yes, it would be another 11 years but he wanted to be remembered. He gave two towns in Utah 500 books each with which they both established libraries. In return, the town of Thurber became Bicknell and the town of Grayson became Blanding, his wife's maiden name.

Nathanael Greene Herreshoff (March 18, 1848 - June 2, 1938) was a monster in the early days of the America's Cup. If you were on a boat he designed between 1893 and 1920, you won. Interesting for a guy who started off not thinking sailboats were his thing.

He graduated from MIT and worked for a steamer company in Pennsylvania. While there, he helps design the first torpedo boat. He returns to Rhode Island to form a business with his brother. He's the boat guy; his brother is the business guy. Along the way, he will get a little too aggressive with one of the steam engines. It will explode and kill a fellow worker. He loses his steamer license over that.

The incident plus a change in the marketplace gets him into sailboats. Turns out it's more fun making luxury craft for those with lots of money than it is competing for defense industry dollars on top engines that can explode.

Vigilant, Defender, Columbia, Reliance, and Resolute are all his. If his designs interest you, you can always stop by the Herreshoff Marine Museum. That's where you can see an early example of a crosscut sail. Because cotton does what it does under pressure, he had to find a solution to stay competitive.

Pasquale Abruzzi (August 29, 1932 - June 3, 1998) is a reminder of a time gone by. In the 40's and 50's, football in Rhode Island was a big deal. Mr. Abruzzi was a running back worthy of mention.

"Pat" or "Doc" was born in Warren and played for their high school team. He was named to the All Class C team in 1948 and 1949. Pat also excelled in baseball as a catcher. He led the Warren/Bristol American Legion baseball team to the Eastern United States Regional Championship in 1949.

His career continued into college. He set University of Rhode Island rushing records and was the Rhode Island Athlete of the year in 1954. Because he did not want to take the winter off, he became a "trampoline performer" during college basketball season.

His career would continue in the Canadian Football League where he played for the Montreal Alouettes. When he retired, he returned to Warren as the High School football coach in the 60's, 70's and 80's. He is a member of both the Rhode Island Football Coaches Hall of Fame and the URI Athletic Hall of Fame.

Do You Know – East Bay?

One thing that makes the East Bay stick out in Rhode Island is how folks use the water. On Aquidneck Island and in the West Bay, the water is often about getting away from it all or out and out showing off. In the East Bay, the water is about getting your head back together and a way of life. This is rather noticeable at Grinnell's Beach in Tiverton. Kinda rocky, waves only happen when a boat goes by and in the old days, there was a line you couldn't go past without getting waved back in by the lifeguard. While all these things are true, it's always crowded in the summertime.

Right down on Main Road with a great view of Portsmouth and Addams Island. Our parents always called it Snake or Rat Island when we were kids. I think that was their way of keeping us from going out there. Little did they know that only made it more attractive.

Fogland Beach is down on the South side of Fogland Point, you'll find this favorite of kayakers and windsurfers. Like other spots, you can see Portsmouth but the view is much more sweeping. The beach features a conservation area with hiking trails and a nature preserve. It is an ideal spot for self-reflection.

South Shore Beach is all about making memories while playing. Splash in the water, play on the sand, feel the sun beam down on you and your and your family. It is a little further south in Little Compton. Technically it's located on the outer edges of Buzzards Bay. This is why you'll see fishermen late night and early morning surfcasting for striped bass. Have you ever grilled a striped bass over an open fire? That experience is worth the trip all by itself.

The beach is next door to a preserve and that is why you might see a number of exotic birds overhead or fishing in the waves. If you head down in the wintertime, be ready for some noise because the local seals occasionally have meetings.

Goosewing Beach Preserve is what happens when you drive by the beach. Yes, parking is going to be close to $30 this year, but all the wildlife interactions you're going to witness make it worth it. Due to the endangered piping plover considering the Preserve to be home, dogs are not allowed in the summertime.

In the modern era, there are a number of vacation rentals within walking distance just in case the great drive isn't your thing. Most have a view of Quicksand Pond. Once again, self-reflection in the face of incredible nature is a worthwhile activity.

The Narragansett Sailing School located in Barrington, is the way to take advantage of the "get into yourself" mindset on the war. They teach cruising, not going fast. The experience is so compelling that many local hotels advertise themselves as being just a few minutes from the sailing school. The best thing about the school is you do not have to own a boat to benefit from their teaching methods. In fact, you might discover "I don't have one yet but I really need to buy a boat" or "Maybe this isn't for me." In any instance, the discovery is going to be honest.

Colt State Park is part of the Poppasquash Farms Historic District in Bristol. It covers over 460 acres. Back in 1905, the Chase, Chuch, and the Van Wickle Farms were consolidated. Most people remember when they've been to the park once they see pictures of Conrad and Pomeroy. Those of the names of the life-size bull statues that "guard the entrance" to the Park on Hope Street.

Whether you hike, run, bike, ride a horse, or have a skateboard that you love, there's a spot in the park for you. The park's fishing pier was refurbished a decade ago for those that get their entertainment while sitting down. A statue of former Rhode Island Senator John Chafee looks over everybody as they come in.

Samuel Pomeroy Colt had the idea of consolidating the farms. "Pom" graduated from MIT and went on to Columbia Law School. He knew the moment he got out of school that politics was his thing. He served in the General Assembly, moved up to Assistant Attorney General, and ended up as Rhode Island Attorney General. Attempts to move up to Governor and Senator later failed.

15

While he realized that perhaps his political path was over, his energy did not wane. Along with the park he also endowed Bristol's high school. Every time you see a Uniroyal Tire he would be the guy to thank.

Nanaquaket Neck is the place to show off on the water. Some people consider it to be the most desirable place to live in Rhode Island. Having grown up in Tiverton, I never considered that I was hanging with my friends across Nanaquaket Bridge. Just about every male child in Tiverton fishes off the Nanaquaket Bridge at some point or another. If you don't catch anything, don't worry as Manchester's Seafood is right next door.

Of course in the early 1900's none of this would have been possible. The entire area was dominated by the Pogy industry. More specifically, by the smell of the Pogy industry. Interesting that Pogy were originally designed as a fertilizer like substitute to help crops grow.

The Tiverton Yacht Club interestingly enough not in Nanaquaket. It is back almost underneath the Sakonnet Bridge. As a kid, some of us would get together with other young people whose parents were at the Yacht Club and more excitedly we would jump off the train escape bridge into the bay. When we got done, there was a famous bait store that also sold snacks under the bridge as well.

Back before the rebuild, the other part of the Yacht Club that was famous was the incredibly steep front staircase. Your parents might have walked gently up the staircase. You had to sprint up them risking life, limb, but more importantly, huge embarrassment if you tripped.

The Sakonnet Yacht Club is a little further south in Little Compton. Because of its location, its members are a little more interested in racing. It was the first place I discovered dinghy racing was a thing.

As I'm writing this, they're looking for a brand new 2023 Sailing Program Director. You'll be responsible for the Junior Sailing Program, Harbor Camp, and Adult Sailing Program. The Yacht Club is so popular that you'll have a staff of almost 30 people. Those who hang around the club regularly will tell you that the way the sea breezes hit, as opposed to other clubs not "facing" the same way, is the biggest attraction.

Roger Williams University proves that how you prepare for what you are going to do is as important as how you spend your recreational time. The University is actually a spinoff of Northeastern in Boston. Northeastern wanted a Southern Branch and started running one in Providence in 1919 inside the YMCA. Fast forward 21 years and now the YMCA is directing the school. In 1956, the university got a charter and in 1969, they bought waterfront property in Bristol.

The school offers programs that include Marine Biology, Masters of Architecture, Historic Preservation, and Construction Management. It is also the only school to offer a Juris Doctor in the entire state.

I have my own history there. Most folks know that I got the speechwriting job working with then Massachusetts State Representative, future State Party Chair, Joan Menard while working at WHTB in Fall River. (Yes, I was there when Rhode Island radio personality Steve Klamkin started his career.) What most folks don't know is that I got the news job at WHTB thanks to being the morning host for Roger Williams in-house rock station WQRI.

The Wharf Tavern wants to remind everybody that whether you want to work, play, or study, you're going to get hungry sooner or later. Because there are so many seafood restaurants in the East Bay by itself, never mind the rest of the state, each one has to take on some style pursuits.

You will first notice that the restaurant is located among historic buildings that date back to the 1800's. Once you walk in, you will immediately take notice of the tall ceilings and large windows. During the warmer months, you do not have to worry about a ceiling at all since you are invited to eat out on the patio. If you stop by, I can vouch for the quality of the grilled swordfish.

Sometimes it's not about a full dinner but just a snack. **The Daily Scoop** has you covered. Take a little ride over to County Road in Barrington during the summer and the ice cream is waiting. What happens if you're further south?

You head to 4 corners and stop by **Gray's Ice Cream** in Tiverton. For 60 years now, they've been a mandatory stop after Little League games. I wonder if folks do that at the Bristol and Fall River locations?

Of course if you drive that far down, you should proceed to 4 Main Street in Adamsville. That location ran from 1778 to 2012. A little while later the General Store closed permanently and an antique shop took over the location. Visiting the location brings happy vibes.

Speaking of things that aren't around anymore but still define the East Bay, a trip to **Balzano's** in Bristol is in order. Back in the 70's and 80's, if mom hadn't cooked a roast, Balzano's was the after-dinner meal. You can visit them at 180 Mount Hope Ave over in Bristol.

All this driving around to look at monuments that used to make you hungry? Can I suggest **Eli's Kitchen** in Warren? Always a highly rated restaurant on the survey sites. Oh wait, that one closed too. The pandemic can be annoying.

Can I ask a question? I know I made you hungry. Are you more hungry for fried seafood or a sit down meal? If your answer is fried seafood and if we've gotten to May, you're going over to **Evelyn's** in Tiverton. Great views of the water as you enjoy your fried clams. Especially busy around noon on Sundays. It does not seem to matter which religious services go on Sundays in the summer. Evelyn's is the stop. From the looks of things, church-going folks also time it so they get there a little after the noon hour.

By the way, have you had lobster chow mein? Have you ever considered lobster chow mein? Yes, they have clam cakes too. However, this is Rhode Island - if I mention somebody's clam cakes, I have to mention remember everybody's clam cakes. Remember how we went viral just before the election?

Oh, you were more in the mood for a sit-down meal that defines the East Bay? Still in Tiverton, drive up to the **Moulin Rouge**. Can I suggest starting with the Jumbo Shrimp? The DaQuay family has owned and operated the establishment for 35 years now. Oh, having a problem finding it? Do the East Bay thing and look for the windmill. The windmill never steers you wrong.

If you really want to understand eating in the East Bay, there is one more restaurant you have to try. **Leo's Ristorante** in Bristol is in its 3rd generation. Not surprisingly, it is the definition of family style. You have to try the chicken parm sandwich.

Before you start thinking everything in the East Bay is all sunshine, I have some examples of where it is not. If you do not present the sketchy and the dark as well as the fun, you're not being honest. If you're "protecting" the residents in this way, you are not being respectful.

Have you heard about **the RI Slave History Medallion** controversy? The RI Slave History Medallion folks like installing their monuments where slaves were trafficked. Newport, RI was the site of a lot of auctioning. Often, slaves bought there were brought by boat to other spots in the East Bay. Back in 2020, the words "In memory of the slaves and their descendants who faithfully served Barrington families" not only freaked out some residents but members of the Barrington Cemetery Commission.

The Slave Medaillon organization is very precise about their language. They also go to great lengths to match the language of the time when the slaves were here. The situation got resolved when another monument was added.

Rhode Island, and especially the East Bay, can have problems when it remembers old times. This is a place where a lot of creepiness was displayed over time. This is an area that is rather liberal now. Getting the two to meld together can be difficult.

Another example of this is when it was time to sell the **Nonquit School.** In the 1950's they went to build a gymnasium and 15 skeletons were discovered. There's now question that the property was an Indian burial ground. It was pretty obvious that the school should have been turned back over to the original owners." Instead, it was sold for what seems like a steal price now.

Sometimes the disagreements are about people who are much more recent to modern times. **Mai Donohue** is a great example. She had an incredible life as part of a political family in the 50's. She came to the United States and married Brian Donohue. They had kids and took in other Vietnamese children seeking direction. She got her GED while living in Barrington and learned how to cook American dishes and Portuguese bread.

What nobody knew about until her daughters went to college is how much racism she faced in the United States and how much she had to hide about her own history. As a method of protection, she hid everything from her own kids. She did not tell them about being politically targeted at an early age. She did not tell them about the racism in Massachusetts that caused her to move to Rhode Island. She did not tell her kids about the racism in Rhode Island that caused her to hide her past from her own offspring. Aren't we supposed to treat visitors better than that?

Another gentleman from the East Bay who understood folks sometimes hid the truth was **Frederick Peck**. He was born in the late 1600's in Providence, and spent most of his time at the family homestead in Barrington. He started as a State Representative and ended up as the State Commissioner of Finances. His favorite thing to do was to collect historical papers.

He had the historic mansion in Barrington named **Belton Court** built. That's where he would read the papers and discover that what many politicians said in public but believed in private, at even the lowest levels, were two different things. Anyone thinking about getting into politics should probably read Mr. Peck's collection of letters from George Washington.

One of the cool things about the East Bay that you learn quickly is whenever conflict arises, there are plenty of historical examples to learn from. The **Coggeshall Farm Museum** in Bristol is one such an example. On 48 acres, you see how farm life would have been in 1799. When you strip things down like that, all of a sudden all your decisions are easier to make. Somehow we forget that minus the technology, someone before us has faced every choice we have to make.

Some folks do not get all theoretical when making a decision. They'd rather go out with friends, listen to music, and then go with the vibe. Over in Warren, the **Galactic Theater** is a perfect place to get in touch with what you need to via music. It should be noted that the food is way underrated.

If looking at the beauty in someone else's creation is your thing, **Blithewold Mansion** is a great place to take that in. On 10 acres, you can experience 300 species of plants. **John DeWolf** designed that "summer retreat" for **Augustus and Bessie Van Wickle** back in the 1890's. Not only can you stand next to Magnolias and Redwoods, you can discover where Ginkgo Biloba comes from. Just taking in the smells can clear your head.

Because they're close by, you can smell all the trees and then head out to Prudence Island via the Prudence Island Ferry on the same day. While Prudence Island is part of Portsmouth and technically is in the West Bay, when you're out there the feel is very much East Bay. A lot of that might be a result of everything being destroyed on the island in the '38 hurricane, except for the general store that doubles as a post office and a school. As a kid growing up in the East Bay what did I learn from the most? You have to walk the **Bristol 4th of July Parade Route**. It helps if you meet some of the business owners. Remember I talked about jumping off the train escape bridge? Those are connected to train tracks that are connected through Tiverton into Fall River. It was a great place to catch frogs and do other things we didn't want our parents to find out about. I'm also going to suggest one more time that you walk the paths around Fort Barton and try the bike path from Bristol to Providence. Once you do all that, you'll understand the feelings the East Bay inspires.

Question: Where is this stone structure located?
Answer on page 161

All About Aquidneck Island

The moment someone hears the words "Aquidneck Island" they think Newport for good reason. A lot of people believe that Newport "carries" the rest of the island if not the entire state. It doesn't work that way. In fact politically, Newport relies on its neighbors to get things done. Because my father worked for the Naval Undersea Service Center (NUSC) which is now the Naval Undersea Warfare Center (NUWC) I learned this at an early age. I have to thank the SUBROC and Tomahawk missiles for letting me know a lot. The rest of what I knew at an early age came from my mom getting mad, with a few other coworkers, at her beauty shop in Middletown and opening up a new salon in Newport. In 1985, I'd "move" to Astor's Beechwood but more on that in a little bit.

The crazy thing is that multiple celebrities rent houses every year in Jamestown and nobody has any idea that they're there. I suppose if you have that kind of money, paying a toll every day, provided you've pre-arranged a place to park, is not that big of a deal. I remember the days when we thought the $2 Newport Bridge toll was expensive. This was especially true if you were dating a young lady who went to University of Rhode Island. Going to Newport was great to impress but you always had to put $2 aside. Digging change out of the glove compartment was never a good look.

Aquidneck Island was originally settled by the Narragansett Indian Tribe. They nicknamed it the "Isle of Peace." They actually called it

23

Aquidnet which became Aquidneck but even Roger Williams and his crew wasn't sure what that meant. In 1638, they sold it to English settlers coming through from Portsmouth. The Island in general has been through many periods of different kinds of settlement. It seems to be the Dutch who said, "Ya know, this whole Aquidneck thing is cool and all but the island is really red from the clay to the foliage so you should call it Roode Island." Other explorers thought the upper section had an "Isle of Rhodes" feel. Combine the two and you get where we are.

By 1750, Rhode Island was a major trade center. Aquidneck Island attracted everyone who is being persecuted for their religious beliefs. It is starting to become an interesting mix. That combination is one major downside. Rhode Island is becoming a major slave trading center filled with auctions and everything.

Slavery isn't the only thing developing. Rhode Islanders in the 1700's are starting to have an attitude. It became the first state, pushed by Aquidneck Island activities, to declare independence from King George in 1776. It was one of those, "Oh, you thought the burning of the Gaspee 4 years ago was cool? Watch this. . . . ."

This need to say "watch this" is going to show up again in the 1850's. Tycoons, mostly from New York but a few from Philadelphia, are going to ask George Champlin Mason to design them a "Summer Cottage." Most folks call these Mansions. Don't worry, we will talk about the ones you can tour, the ones with séances in them, the ones famous from certain kinds of parties, the ones where the need to do drugs was movie- like, and even the one I lived in for a summer.

Not everything on Aquidneck Island was about showing off. Sometimes it was about taking care of your neighbors. Jewish folks are always getting persecuted by somebody. This was also true back in the 1750's. Rhode Island, and Aquidneck Island especially, was a beacon for religious freedom. Due to the events coming together the Touro Synagogue was built between 1759 and 1763. You can still visit it today. Some politicians in Newport have thought of it as being a good luck charm and visit the Synagogue before making a major speech or attending a meeting. The Synagogue was named for Issac Touro, the first officiating Rabbi.

The folks living on Aquidneck Island did not have to do much to develop other industries outside of merchant and slave trading. The Narragansett Indians had done all the work for them. The need to manage the land the same way, including horse and chicken farms, became clear early. So did the bountiful fishing stock.

Some people figured out that between all the business travel and the rich folks starting to show for the oceans meant that you could open a small business and you wouldn't have to worry about a customer base. The John Stevens Shop specializes in description and one of a kind inscription on stone. They were opened in 1705. They still are and have a worldwide clientele. They also bring in the "curiosity" spinoff customers, and you wondered how timeshares became popular, who arrive by the millions every summer.

If you do visit Aquidneck Island, there are a few photo opportunities you shouldn't miss. The beaches will also have their own section so we'll let them be for now. There are 3 bridges that connect Aquidneck Island to the rest of the world. Taking pictures from the Portsmouth side of the Mount Hope and Sakonnet Bridges is amazing. Most experienced travelers come in this way, avoiding the mess that the Newport Bridge can be once you get into town, but they forget to go back and get the pics on the way out. The Newport Bridge looking out is amazing. However, most internet maps tell you to drive in that way and many folks grab a snapshot on the way here.

There is one last little place you should visit. It gets very little attention from non-islanders. Folks who live on Aquidneck Island often visit to achieve "peace." After certain cemeteries, we'll get into that later, it has always been a big inspiration for me. You know, you're driving up Memorial Boulevard, you cross Bellevue Avenue, you pass Sardella's, you start to go down the hill where the Cliff Walk starts, you start down the hill and Easton Beach is on your right. Look to your left. That's Easton Pond. Make sure you find the stone path. Take the smells in. I would tell you to fish but they change the rules all the time so check in with a local bait shop before you do that. Enjoy the quiet, the peace, the knowledge of everything that surrounds you. If you know Aquidneck Island, this stop is definitely on your list.

People of Significance – Aquidneck Island

Anne Hutchinson (July 20, 1591 - August 20, 1643) is just not putting up with anyone's nonsense. She was a Puritan Spiritual advisor and a religious reformer with a nose for controversy. Ask the folks in the Massachusetts Bay Colony.

Her parents made sure she had a better education than most other girls ever dreamed of achieving. Her need to walk the way she talked caused the Antinomian Controversy. That got her tossed from Massachusetts. Thankfully she was in touch with Roger Williams. He invited her down to Portsmouth. In later years, people would back and realize she was probably one of the United States' most important female colonists. Her tenacity was something that inspired many to seek freedom.

William Coddington (1601 – November 1, 1678) is a major reason why Rhode Island is the way it is. He too started out in the Massachusetts Bay Colony. He too got caught up in the Antinomian Controversy. He served as a judge in Portsmouth and Newport then became the Governor of both Portsmouth and Newport and then Governor of the entire Colony.

In 1647, **Roger Williams** had gone to England to unite Narragansett, Warwick, Portsmouth, and Newport. Portsmouth and Newport wanted no part of this. He got named the Governor of all 4, but then didn't want the gig. He was replaced by **Jeremy Clarke**. Mr. Coddington got so ticked off that he went to England and lobbied for a "patent" to separate Newport and Portsmouth from the deal. He was successful and this could have gone on for an indefinite period.

That went well for a little while but the mainland town didn't like the way he was running things. Cell phones and emails didn't exist yet so Roger Williams, Jeremy Clarke, and William Dyer had to go back to England to straighten out the mess. They were successful lobbying for their patent. Coddington withdrew from public life a year later and became a member of the Religious Society of Fiends.

Two decades went by. In 1673, he came back as the Lieutenant Governor and took the top job, 1 year terms, from 1674-1676. Unfortunately, the **King Philip's War** hit in 1675 making a mess out of things. He lost to **Benedict Arnold**. Bet you didn't know there was a Benedict Arnold this early. He would die in 1678. When Governor Arnold died, Governor Coddington got elected one more time, and people nowadays complain when politicians run multiple times, but unfortunately died a few years later. He is buried in **Coddington Cemetery** over in Newport.

Benedict Arnold (December 21, 1615 - June 19, 1678) is not the Benedict Arnold you think it is. It is his Granddaddy. Yes, that's right, Benedict Arnold the Traitor's Grandad was Governor of Rhode Island.

He too was born in England. He too settled in the Massachusetts Bay Colony. Guess what caused him to leave? Sure enough Roger Williams reaches out to him and he settles in Pawtuxet which is now Cranston. While he's there, he studied all the native languages and because a leading interpreter. In 1651, he leaves Pawtuxet and heads to Newport. In 1657, he becomes President of the Colony. In 1662, he becomes President again. In 1663, the Royal Charter showed up and magically he became Governor. When Governor Coddington was not Governor, he was. That whole "Let's go to England and get a new patent" thing had to be really annoying when you were in office. He would die in office and leave his "stone built windmill" to his wife. That shall become an important Rhode Island landmark.

Bishop George Berkeley (March 12, 1685 - January 14, 1753) was born into a wealthy Irish family. He always had a desire to travel. At an early age, he had already explored some of Europe and Bermuda. In 1728, he accepted a salary of 100 pounds a year and headed to Newport. He settled in what is now Middletown establishing the Whitehall Plantation. He is another big slavery guy so sometimes he drifts into the background when we talk about history. For instance, most people do not know that Bishop Berkeley is responsible for bringing John Smibert to America. The Bishop discovered the "Scottish artist" while on a trip to Italy. Mr. Smibert will become the father of American portrait painting.

Bishop Berkeley, even with all the travel experience, is best known for his theories on existence. As a philosopher, he advanced a theory he called immaterialism. Others will refer to it as subjective idealism. While in his time it did not attract many, it will become a major tool in the philosophy world after World War II. Many have studied and promoted his ideas while not realizing every time they traveled by Whitehall in Middletown, they were right next to where many of the ideas were constructed.

Ida Lewis (February 25, 1842 - October 24, 1911) was born in Newport. Her dad was transferred to the Lighthouse service and appointed keeper of Lime Rock Light. Soon after, he suffered a stroke. Ida found herself taking care of the house, helping out mom, and doing dad's job at night.

By the age of 15, she was considered to be the best swimmer in Newport. Because dad's lighthouse was surrounded by water, that was kind of important.

Eventually her mom died too and Ida took over the lighthouse duties as the actual caregiver instead of just doing the work. At $750 a year, she was the highest paid lighthouse keeper in the country. She was officially credited with saving eighteen lives in her career. Many folks around town at the time would tell you the real number was 25.

Many Presidents and Admirals would honor her. The Suffrage movement celebrated her achievements demonstrating how strong women could be. In a way, she became Newport's first tourist attraction. One year, nine thousand people came to visit her. When she died in 1911 due to a stroke, 1400 went to the Thames Street Methodist Church to view her body.

In 1924, Lime Rock became Ida Lewis Rock. Following that path, the Lime Rock Lighthouse became the Ida Lewis Lighthouse. It is now the Clubhouse of the Ida Lewis Yacht Club. The 18 stars you see repre-sent the 18 folks she saved. Many political insiders will tell you more political deals go down there than at the Newport or New York yacht Clubs.

She has a road named after her and a few bands have said she in-spired them to write songs about her. The USCGC Ida Lewis is stationed in Middletown. In 1995, the US Coast Guard named a class of buoy ten-ders after her. It seems that every year, someone's dedication to her turns into a positive act.

John Jacob Astor IV (July 13, 1864 - April 15, 1912) and I have partied a lot in the same house. But that is because I lived there. More on that later.

Mr. Astor had $87 million when he died. That is the equivalent of almost $3 billion today. He was born in New York and served in the military. He also authored novels. When not doing that, he loved real estate and was responsible for the Astoria Hotel.

His personal life was out of a modern-day soap opera. He got mar-ried. Then he got divorced due to a 19-year-old young lady. Then he married the 19-year-old young lady at Astor's Beechwood. No, I never told that story while I was "working" there.

He makes the list out of all the Astors due to his dying on the Titanic. It's not so much his dying on the boat - it's the way Hollywood and even the Nazis have treated the legends about him being on the boat. He ends up in all the films with Eric Braeden playing him in the most recent ver-sion. Whether he is supposedly rescuing dogs or giving a little boy a hat so people think he's a little girl and therefore can get on the lifeboat first, the stories are never ending. Yes, he has a key role in the Mansions section.

John Huston (August 5, 1906 - August 28, 1987) was an American film director. He wrote most of the screenplays for the thirty-seven plays he directed. Those would include The Maltese Falcon, The Treasure of the Sierra Madre, The Asphalt Jungle, The African Queen, The Man Who Would Be King, and Prizzi's Honor.

Huston's life was marked by his alcoholism. He was a drifter who killed a young lady in a drunk driving accident. He was also a genius who mastered how to tell an audience about 2 people going on a quest in visual form. At the end, he just wanted rest and peace before he died due to lung disease complications. When his rich friends would invite him to Newport, he would always think of Middletown as that "soft, restful" place. Based on that, he rented a house in Middletown and spent his last years there.

Billy Gonsalves (August 10, 1908 - July 17, 1977) was born long before American soccer was as popular as it is now. Back when he was born, it was all about where you grew up. He was born in Portsmouth and grew up between Portsmouth and Fall River, MA.

By the time he was done, he was considered to be the Babe Ruth of American Soccer at a time when many did not know American soccer really existed. Not only would he set records playing the game he loved, he was part of the first two United States World Cup teams.

Doris Duke (November 22, 1912 - October 28, 1993) when you get down to it, was a tobacco heiress. The important part is she knew how to have fun and help others. At times, she was the "richest girl in the world".

A lot of Newport would not exist without her. She was the Founder of the Newport Restoration Foundation. She understood that by making Jacqueline Kennedy Onassis a star via a vice presidency in the organization, every door would open. Following the doors, wallets would open.

She knew she liked art and traveling. She loved animals and became a wildlife refuge supporter. She loved sports and learned how to surf. Did I mention she was 6 feet tall? She not only helped preserve homes, she jumped on the ladder and did some of the work.

I will save the car accident for the Mansion section. For now, kindly remember that Ms. Duke sought out and made bedroom partners out of Errol Flynn and George S. Patton, among others. Reportedly, she once paid somebody's wife $1 million so they would get divorced and she would marry the husband.

Her death still brings up questions, like the car accident does, to this day. Was it really the facelift and the hip replacement? Was it suicide? Did somebody get jealous and murder her? If I meet her on the other side, I am definitely asking.

Claiborne Pell (November 22, 1918 - January 1, 2009) is a person we will never fully understand. Long before his political career, he was literally on the battlefield helping out those fighting against the Nazis on Nazi turf. He was captured, and later released several times.

Most people do not know that he authored 3 books. They also do not know that he was awarded 50 honorary degrees. The Newport Bridge was renamed the Pell Bridge after him.

When we get to his political career, only 2 words need be said: Pell Grants. When was the last time anyone ever said Basic Education Opportunity Grant? When not doing that, he served as Chair of the Foreign Relations Committee for 8 years.

He had a taste for the paranormal and superstition. You have to be mighty superstitious to wear a belt that fits someone twice your size. He also had a fondness for late night activities which is where the phrase "jogging with Senator Pell" comes from. The phrase became so popular that in the mid 80's, literally a 100 of us would go running together on Bellevue Avenue early in the morning wondering if we would spot him.

Gloria Vanderbilt (February 20, 1924 - June 17, 2019) is another example of "it's not where you live sometimes but rather where you do interesting things". Most of her fashion and writing life took place outside of Newport. She was very New York.

However, when it was time to have romantic trysts with Frank Sinatra, Marlon Brando, Howard Hughes, or Ronald Dahl, where do you go? You got to the Breakers. When you need to teach your son, Anderson Cooper, some things in a quiet place, where do you go? You go to the Breakers. When you want to write a book, you go to the Breakers. When you need to get over a divorce, you go to the Breakers.

31

Rhode Island for the rich can be a 4-month experiment some years at best. The trait that runs through everyone on this path is that special activities are always saved for the summer up here instead of the warm winter place down there. When Cornelius Vanderbilt is your dad that can happen. If that were not true, many of us never would have met Anderson Cooper as kids.

Claus Von Bulow (August 11, 1926 – May 25, 2019) was a Danish born British lawyer. Most of his life will be spent outside of Newport until he decides to become famous in 1982. In one of the first modern celebrity trials with TV, his wife Sunny is in a coma supposedly caused by Claus. At the time, my mom co-owned Coiffeur-sur-mer which was located in what is now a bed and breakfast behind the Jane Pickens Theater. I had a choice each day - go to Bishop Connolly or hang out by the courthouse. Which one do you think I picked most days?

Claus would be found guilty in the first trial. What most folks don't know was that Alan Dershowitz was already watching the proceedings. A bunch of us somewhat knew who he was and idolized him back then. We would never say that today. It should be noted that Cosima Von Bulow was already beautiful back then.

Claus then would hire Attorney Dershowitz, win an appeal, and then win the second trial. That's when I got a chance, through a buddy, to help cut the lawn at Clarendon Court. The only thing more famous than the trial was the victory party which was pitched at a thank-you event. Supposedly, Norman Mailer lifted up the curtain at that one. To this day, most Newporters around from the time still think Claus is guilty. However, when 8 medical experts help you out at trial, you usually win.

Dorrance Hamilton (August 16, 1928 - April 18, 2017) and I used to fight like cats and dogs when I lived in Newport from 2001-2012. I got along with her handpicked Council member Kate Leonard great but our goals were just different.

"Dodo" was the Campbell's Soup heiress. She founded the SVF Foundation and helped save Hammersmith Farm. While many of us fought with her constantly about planning and zoning issues, she was always available for questions.

I think that was the best part about her. While the crew I hung with had a totally different vision for Newport, mostly because many of us were in the hospitality business, she was always there to explain and teach. I learned an amazing amount from her. Even though she drove me crazy, seeing the revitalization of Queen Anne Square, I miss her now. When I went to Utica, I'd take some of the things she'd say and refit them. You have no idea how easy it is to compete against non-millionaires until you've done nothing but compete against billionaires for a decade.

Larry Ellison (August 17, 1944 - Present) is the co-founder of Oracle. He is setting himself up to be a huge part of Newport's future. Mr. Ellison is a yacht racing guy with his current home base in San Francisco.

In 2010, he purchased Astors' Beechwood. We'll talk about that in the Mansions section. Now, it looks like his wife has been working on a museum for some time. In 1919, he purchased the Seacliff home. He now owns all 4 properties between Rosecliff and Marble House. Perhaps more than one museum is on the table.

Sheldon Whitehouse (October 20, 1955 - Present) started by winning the Attorney General race, ran for Governor which he lost, then won the race for Senator. He is also part of my recovery story as we had an amazing conversation the week before I famously got sober.

Most famously when Sheldon was the US Attorney, having been picked by Bill Clinton, he ran Operation Thunderdome which led to Buddy Cianci's arrest. He was also in charge of the extortion conviction of Gerard Ouimette.

Sheldon's biggest controversies come from the fact that certain Beach Clubs and Yacht Clubs haven't gotten the diversity thing down yet. Yes, there are supposedly nonwhite members at Bailey's but you can't tell that from the outside. I know a number of Bailey's members and they're not a racist crew per se. A little snotty and picky? Yes. Racist? No. I just wish they'd take my suggestion of involving a couple of hip hop stars to join and then everybody would get over it.

Michael Flynn (December 24, 1958 - Present) is probably the most controversial name on this list. If you are a Trump supporter, he and by extension his son General Charles Flynn, are great Americans making sure the Deep State cannot achieve its goals. If you are everybody else, he committed treason on January 6th, hangs out with all kinds of fringe right racists as well, never mind trying to trust his son. Life was much different before Trump showed up.

Before Trump, Mike Flynn was a counterterrorism expert who served as a National Security advisor. No one really questioned him. When his military career ended, there were a few dark nights at the Clarke Cooke House when he might have talked more than he should but who hasn't done that?

I remember Mike Flynn from Middletown. I remember the kid we looked up to because he helped save two children when somebody else's mom set their parking brake incorrectly. He has a Master of Arts in National Security and Strategic Studies from the Naval War College. He was on the path you wanted to follow.

Now, he's a crazy Q-anon guy wondering if most of us are half lizards. Worse, he might have helped plan January 6th. Whether he wants to be remembered for that or the highly decorated guy he also is will be up to him.

Peter Neronha (December 17, 1963 - Present) is Rhode Island's Attorney General. He grew up in Wakefield and later on moved to Jamestown. Ok, admit it - even if you live in Rhode Island, you had no idea he called Jamestown home, did you?

Jack Reed and Sheldon Whitehouse lobbied very vigorously to get him named as US Attorney back in 2009. He normally plays bigger roles behind the scenes. For instance some people can tell you about his cases but can they tell you how he co-chaired the Office of Management and Budget on behalf of the Department of Justice? Most people don't know how instrumental he was regarding reigning in offshore pharmacies.

When he gets criticized, it comes down in one of two areas. He is thought to be too protective of cops. He did let someone drive into a protest once. He also sometimes "protects the house" a little too much regarding the Open Meetings Law and access to Public Records in General. However, most voters are law and order types. He does well there so he is liked.

We may find out in two years how loved he is because as I write this, there are rumors of him running for Governor in 2026. He would tell you he still has a lot of work to do regarding pedophilia and the Providence Diocese. He would also tell you there's some firearm legislation he would like to see passed.

Tanya Donelly (July 14, 1966 - Present) founded the Throwing Muses with her stepsister. She was also in the Breeders and became the front person for Belly. You might remember their hit "Feed the Tree." She spent her early life rotating, literally, between California and Newport while her parents tried to figure things out.

Yes, she and I have met although I doubt she would remember me. Back in 1985, Throwing Muses played UMass-Dartmouth, still SMU at the time. I was reviewing the band for the student newspaper The Torch. The show wasn't that great, and she shot me down. It was a rough review. However, the band rebounded, and I was a huge fan of her work through the 80's and 90's. Then you think things have gone by until you find out she wrote the score for the animated film Luck.

Charlie Day (February 9, 1976 - Present) would have never made this list before 2005. He was just a guy who grew up in Middletown. Then *It's Always Sunny in Philadelphia* hit, and he is one of the funniest guys on TV ever.

His dad is a music teacher at Salve Regina in Newport. I bet those students have some stories. His mom taught piano at the Penfield School. I guess that is where the musical talent came from. It was just recently announced that Charlie will be doing the voice of Luigi in the Super Mario Bros. Movie coming out in a few months,

I think you can see a theme in this list. People come from somewhere else, arrive in Newport, create memories, and then have to stay. I know that feeling all too well as I travel on in my life. Once again, if you think

I missed somebody, and I am sure some of you do, don't be afraid to hit me up with an email and tell me why.

Do You Know – Aquidneck Island?

One of the coolest things about living on Aquidneck Island is because so many celebrities visit, you never know where or when you are going to make a memory. They have this ability to pop out of nowhere next to a building you never expected. That happened to me on a weekday night in 2012.

I went for a run. On the way back, there was this building which had been a bank branch which at that time was a club. Tom Morello was working on an indie project and he had his band in town. He was standing outside. Living in Newport, you learn how to quickly approach celebrities and not embarrass yourself. I went up to thank him just for *Rage Against the Machine* because I loved them so much. We ended up having a half hour conversation about life and politics.

If you are wondering because you've heard the story, yes, later on that night I got grabbed on Thames Street. I was still walking on my way back home, as a 45- year-old I just ran 3 and walked 3 back, as the bars were closing. Two young women approached me. They explained they were in a competition against two of their friends across the road to see who could grab the most guys. I was in decent shape for a 45-year-old at the time and have been told I'm cute, but I'm still waiting for the punch-line. So I said "go ahead" so they could continue with their prank.

Turns out, she reaches down and grabs me. That was shocking enough. However, it got really entertaining when her friend threw her hands in the air, screamed, and celebrated like they scored a touchdown during the playoffs. They won the bet. I can't imagine those two events happening back to back on a weekday night anywhere else but Thames Street.

I suppose if you wanted to have that kind of experience between 1830 and 1890, you would have headed to the Old Beach Road Historic District. If you couldn't afford a mansion and an expensive architect but still had money in the bank, you built to the North of Memorial Boulevard instead of the South. That neighborhood still has work every day but in an office feel.

In that neighborhood, you will notice some folks know how to sneak out without running into a great number of tourists. For many Newporters, there are always two options to everything. The first is the popular option that everybody knows about. The second is a location that offers the same benefits with less tourists and more quiet. That explains the popularity of Sachuest Point.

242 acres by the water draws almost 70,000 visitors per year. It started as a horse racing spot, became a spot for Naval communications, and now is host to a wildlife refuge. While the fishing is awesome, the Harlequin Ducks end up in the most photos.

The Audubon Society granted the 242 acres back in 1970 which was developed into a wildlife reserve. That was a big change from its original military role. You had to stop the enemy from coming up the Sakonnet River somehow.

Fort Adams was established in July 1799 in case somebody did hit land. It was named for President John Adams. What we see today was development between 1824 and 1857. Its biggest role in our history would arrive a few years later.

During the Civil War, the government was worried that some folks from Maryland might end up on the wrong side of the war. For that reason, the U.S. Naval Academy was moved to Fort Adams temporarily.

Even after the Naval Academy went back home, the Fort had a role in defending the Sakonnet River and Narragansett Bay until 1965. The property had been transferred back to the Army in 1953. Until the 1970s, the Fort fell into a state of disrepair. Then the folks from The Scarlet Letter wanted to use the Fort as a filming location. Suddenly, everyone realized the potential the Fort had. By 1995, tours were the order of the day.

People are also surprised that the **International Tennis Hall of Fame** went through a period of disrepair. In 1879, **James Gordon Bennett Jr.** wanted to create an exclusive establishment where wealthy summer residents could play. **Charles McKim** designed the exterior in the Shingle Style and **Stanford White** designed the interiors. Originally it was the Tennis Club and the Casino Theatre.

The **United States Lawn Tennis Association** held their first championship at the Newport location in 1881. That would go on until 1914 and then World War I got in the way. By the 1950's things were looking rough as the marketplace had changed. In 1954, Jimmy and Candy Van Alen put new money into the facility, also establishing the museum. Almost immediately, the United States Tennis Association sanctioned the museum. It was recognized by the International Tennis Association in the mid 80's. The memorabilia collection is always growing.

Interestingly, the **Old Stone Mill** has never been in a state of disrepair. It was erected in the mid-17th century. Conspiracy theorists are always positing that it got here much earlier but science always disproves that. If we could give credit to the Knights Templar or the Vikings someday, that would be awesome. What cannot be disproven is that certain windows line up with certain stars. In case you are wondering, yes folks have jumped the fence and engaged in romantic trysts inside of the Tower.

Conspiracy theorists are also always speculating on Diane Drake's death. One minute in 1980 she is walking down Easton's Beach at age 19. The next minute, her body is being discovered. She had been strangled. Because of which celebrities were in town at the time, speculation mounts.

Had this happened back in the late 1600's, we could have blamed this on Captain Kidd. He claimed that somewhere on the banks of the Sakonnet River in what is now Portsmouth a great treasure awaits. All you need is a metal detector and a shovel.

Makes you wonder if Captain Kidd ever visited the White Horse Tavern? It opened in 1673 and is America's oldest restaurant. Amazing food, great service, fantastic location. William Coddington had a brother-in-law named Francis Brinley. In 1652, Governor Coddingtown loaned over the piece of land and Mr. Brinley sat on the property for 20 years after building a barn. In 1673, William Mayes bought the property and enlarged the structure to be a full tavern. It also was to serve as a meeting room and city hall of sorts. Jonathan Nichols took over the property in 1730 and calls it **The White Horse Tavern**.

British troops were quartered there during the Revolution. Then it served as a boarding house in 1952. Van Buren donated money to the Preservation Society. A restaurant was born.

I know the Tavern well because I used to live behind it. In fact, which is where I was living the night, I got sober. That was preceded a couple of weeks earlier by the night I removed a couple of mattresses from the basement and then drunkenly danced around them like I had hit the lottery. The police officers sitting in the Tavern parking lot at the time found it to be quite entertaining.

In a way, what the police officers experienced is one of the best things about Aquidneck Island. You don't have to be directly at the scene; just next to is good enough. For instance, as a visitor you will never be a part of the largest sector of the local economy after tourism. That is military contracting.

As you drive across the island, especially by business parks in Middletown and Portsmouth, you will be right next to folks helping design the next weapon. You can work directly for the military, like my dad did, or you can work for a contractor like many family members, and I have. Without the military contractors, the housing isn't the same and many small businesses can't survive. Even tourism has its limits.

Would you be surprised if you found out most of the kids of the contractors end up at the same schools? That is what I found out at Saint Philomena's and Portsmouth Abbey. They are both located in Portsmouth literally 400 feet away from each other and around the corner from Green Animals. To be fair, the kids who go to the Abbey, all boys when

I went, have parents who run the firms while the kids at St. Phil's have parents who work at the firms. I swear some of my classmates my freshman year in high school had more money than my parents.

Portsmouth Abbey was founded in 1926 by the Benedictines. It is a day and boarding school. Its goal is to prepare you for the Board Room. (On the other hand, the Jesuits, when they had Jesuits, at Bishop Connolly prepared you for the political backroom.) You can tell by the alumni list, which includes Sean Spicer and Jim Farley, that the Abbey is doing a great job.

When you attend **St. Philomena's**, you are introduced to the Faithful Companions of Jesus. Looking at the campus now, it is amazing that this all started as one little building. I wonder if the kids still play the "throw the tennis ball at the curb and try to get it to land on the roof for a home run" game?

Back in those days, we often took field trips to **Fort Wetherill State Park.** 62 acres at the tip of Conanicut Island over in Jamestown is hard to beat. In 1776, the Revolutionaries thought Dumpling rock would be a key location to engage in the defense of the Narragansett Bay. During the Revolutionary War, everybody got a turn invading and controlling the site for a little while. When the British evacuated their Newport forces, they deserted Dumpling Rock.

In 1798, the United States military thought a permanent artillery location would be appropriate. Both in 1899 and 1901 this idea was expanded upon. Eventually the state of Rhode Island acquired the property and created a place to watch sailing races that turned into a full park.

Since you're here, you can also visit the beach from **Moonrise Kingdom**. Wes Anderson used Fort Wetherill's beach and many other spots in Rhode Island for his film. In an interesting way, Rhode Island's visual impressions brought out a softer side of Wes Anderson.

As you are really close to the water, look out to the rocks. See that house kind of leaning over? That is **Clingstone House** built in 1905. When you get closer up, you'll realize the shingle style cottage does have

3 floors and 23 rooms. In 1961, the house was bought for $3,600 in back taxes.

Have you had enough fun with the Southern part of the Island yet? One last thing to do. Head to the far north end of the island and check out the Conanicut Island Lighthouse. The Lighthouse hasn't been active since 1934, but it's still a great location from which you can observe the business side of the bay.

2nd and 3rd Beaches in Middletown have always been about watching of another kind. 2nd is really **Sachuest** Beach as you might imagine, aligning with the Point. Out of the 3 local beaches, including Easton's in Newport, this one has the biggest waves. 3rd Beach is much calmer and more about tanning. Hazard's and Gooseberry play a much different role. While they are beaches, they're much more about fishing and crabbing than waves.

If nobody mentions it, you may not realize that the trip from 2nd Beach to **Purgatory Chasm** is just a couple hundred yards or so. Do us both a favor and play, do not try to jump across it. Yes, folks did that years ago but the space between the two sides increases every year. Besides the rocks alone being worth looking at, the Chasm itself is a natural wonder.

A new Newport tourist trend is to schedule beach days in the morning and trips to the Newport Car Museum in the afternoon. Gunther and Maggie Buerman wanted to bring joy and they have. As a young lad, Gunther had a keen interest in car advertisements.

That type of tradition also makes Newport a little different. In most locations, you do whatever during the day and then hit an attraction at night. In Newport, the people in the city with you are the attraction. The center of that attraction tends to be the Wave Statue.

In 1983, Katherine Worden wanted to create an ode to Japanese artist Hokusai. So now feet appear just before they enter the wave. This has led to an interesting winter tradition. On especially cold nights, folks put socks on the feet.

41

My own connection to the **Wave Statue** was that it made me a lot of money between 2006 and 2011. I was the Sales Director at the Newport Bay Club just behind the statue. We know when folks stay at different hotels or are deciding where to eat at night, they always meet at the Wave. It made sense to put up a little booth with a sign that said "directions." 90% of the time, I was just a friendly host making suggestions. Every so often folks would ask, "Hey, what's the least inexpensive way to stay downtown" and a timeshare conversation was in the offing.

It should be noted that some folks come to Aquidneck Island and don't want to deal with humans at all. 583 Third Beach Road is a great spot for them. **The Norman Bird Sanctuary** was established thanks to Mabel Norman Cerio. Some folks do the most amazing things when they die. Handing over 325 acres with more than 7 miles of hiking trails has to be on the list.

Once most folks check things out in the Visitor's Center, they head straight to Hanging Rock. Yes, **Hanging Rock** is an inspiration to many artists of all types. If you want to see celebrities- real early in the morning - on the way home from the party for them, is the time to be there. Amazing what originally started with a farmhouse that featured an unnaturally large chimney.

Another spot you can sometimes spot celebrities trying to have a little time in the quiet but tasty, I don't drink wine but that's what folks tell me, is at **Greenvale Vineyards**. Think exceptional estate grown wines just 5 miles north of the city. Both tastings and tours are available.

Since you are that close, you have to visit **Escobar's Highland Farm** as well. If you live in a suburban or urban environment, you have two choices. You can wait every year for September and go up to Syracuse and talk to the farmers while they sleep next to their cattle and goats. Your other option is to visit the great folks at Escobar's. While the State Fair has taught me too much, it's only once a year. If your NFL team has a bye week, Escobar's is available to you.

Do you believe that inanimate objects can hold onto memories and feelings? **The Wanton-Lyman-Hazard House** does exactly that. Built in 1697, it is the oldest surviving house in Newport.

The home was originally built by Stephen Mumford. It changed hands many times until the **Newport Historical Society** took it over in the 1920s. It's one of the few houses that's had its paint scientifically researched so that it could be restored to the original formula.

I saved **Bailey's Beach Club** for last. If you prefer the Spouting Rock Beach Association, I get it. I have not been there since 2010 so I am sure some things have changed.

What remains as an anomaly is the reputation the club has versus what many of them personally believe. Yes, the club was started to avoid mill workers taking the trolley. If you want to see what that was like, go down to Reject's Beach and use a set of binoculars.

If you meet the folks in the Bailey's Club, you will discover that the great majority of them are socially liberal. They normally confide in Democrats although sometimes they have to contribute to Republicans for "business reasons." Why they don't openly recruit nonwhite folks is just beyond me. Wouldn't it be cool to see 'Lil Baby or Dr. Dre at the beach? Imagine seeing them play volleyball with some of the Buffet's family. That could only happen at Bailey's.

Once again, I apologize to anybody who thinks I left something or someone important out. I am easy to find on social media. Please feel free to hit me up and tell me what I missed.

Question: Can you identify this stadium?
Answer on page 161

All About South County

South County is the Rhode Island name for what really is Washington County. If you live anywhere in the Northeast, so many things are named for Washington that many of them develop a local reference. In the case of South County, we actually know that it was Levi Whipple in 1767 who wanted to differentiate South County from Providence County. To be fair, Washington County was originally King's County.

When folks started showing up on boats in the 1800's, there were 5 Native American Tribes living in South County. It soon became clear that the Narragansett Indians were the most politically adept. You can argue that they cut the deal that led the Peqots to become extinct. It's hard to believe that in the late 1600's, there were close to 6000 Narragansetts living in South County.

Yes, Roger Williams gets all the credit. However, it was Giovanni da Verrazano who pitched the idea of sailing west to the Francis I of France and collected a check. He will be the first European to show up on our shores. Henry Hudson is going to follow in his footsteps. Sadly, along with the jewelry and the cool art the Europeans showed up with, they also brought diseases Native American antibodies weren't ready for. That resulted in a lot of deaths. Makes you wonder if things could have been different if they only had masks? Also tells us that if aliens ever do decide to reveal themselves, we should immediately hand them masks.

A lot of what went on in the early days was almost like a game of calling dibs. Samuel Gorton puts together the Shawomet purchase from the Narragansetts. Then while he was trying to be nice to them, others are engaging in wars that only get held up with the Narragansetts help eliminate another tribe. Literally from day to day in South County during certain parts of its history, you didn't know who or what court was running where you lived. That had to be annoying.

In 1686, James II tried to put an end to all this when he created the Dominion of New England. Nobody likes this on this side of the ocean. In fact, the folks in Massachusetts seem more upset about it than folks living under it do. They really hate Governor Edmund Andros. They hate him so much that they arrest him, totally shaky, and send him back to England. Kings County returns to "part of Rhode Island" form of government.

Even in 1729 when it was incorporated as Kings County, the folks living there would refer to it as Narragansett County. Naming it for George Washington in 1781 did not change what the locals thought. Indian trading posts were established at Fort Neck in Charlestown and Smith's Castle in Wickford. That would greatly influence how and where folks settled in the county.

One thing you learn about South County is if you don't like who is in charge, wait a minute. This was also true due to the Revolutionary War. Because both sides were so interested in Newport, if you wanted to stay hidden while doing sneaky things, you would go in and out of South County. One great example is when Lord Howe was supposed to take 8 ships from New York City to Newport to back up British troops. It \being New England, of course he hit a storm and some of the boats were damaged. He had to pull into Point Judith during the first week of August.

French Admiral Comte d'Estaing was watching the advance. He thought Howe would have an advantage. So he took some of his ships and tried to intercept Howe. The "storm" turned into the summertime version of a Northeaster and all the two fleets could do was maneuver around each other. Meanwhile, Major General John Sullivan thinks the French are right around the block and the clock is ticking on his attack in Newport. What he doesn't know is that the French flagship is barely seaworthy at this point. The French Fleet, after losing three one-on-one sea battles in a row, did some repairs in South County and then took off for Delaware.

The geographic location of South County creates some interesting weather conditions. Yes, winds from the East have to cross Aquidneck Island first. This provides for a much more relaxed atmosphere at the beaches. However, anything from the South, especially wind patterns that come up the West Bay, can create total chaos in a short amount of time.

South County is home to approximately 140,000 Rhode Islanders. The great majority, as in a 94% majority, are white. 76% of the folks living in the area own a home and for those that don't, $1,500 a month is the median rent. One interesting thing you notice going through the statistics is that while 95% of people living here have graduated from high school, only 46% have graduated from college. Usually when the high school rate is that high, the college graduation rate is higher.

The basic marketing pitch in South County goes along the lines of "Everything you love on Aquidneck Island or anywhere in Newport County for that matter, but much more quiet and less crowded." Beaches? Check. Great Restaurants? Check. Awesome places to stay? Check. Celebrity sightings or congested traffic? Not really South County's thing.

It is hard to pick between the Scarborough, Misquamicut, and Narragansett beaches. Once you settle in, you can dig into the sand - western Rhode Island sand is much different than Newport County sand, and take in the sounds of the ocean. That ability to dial into the sounds, smells, and rhythm of nature is the biggest South County offering. When you get done, keep in mind that Point Judith is an active fishing port. That means you can take advantage of "off the boat" pricing on your seafood.

One thing most folks don't know? When you visit the University of Rhode Island Bay Campus, you are actually visiting the location of a

World War II POW Camp. Fort Kearney was established in 1943 at a "DeNazifying" center. The thought was if we teach folks about capitalism and freedom, they'll leave the Nazi Party and become productive citizens, behind barbed wire. The only building that is still left is the Wharf on Bunker Road.

People of Significance – South County

You will notice a pattern whenever we discuss the western half of Rhode Island versus the Eastern half. The folks in the Western want all of the benefits but hate the noise and the crowds the benefits bring. That sometimes results in some very interesting choices.

George Hazard (1700-1738) was a great example of that. He was born into a political family. Without doing a lot of work, he traded up with his family connections, becoming Deputy Governor of the Rhode Island Colony and Providence Plantations. Many of his kids and grandkids would end up with titles like "Mayor of Newport." Even though all that was going on, when he paid his dad one thousand pounds for "Foddering Place," he didn't want anybody else to know.

It's harder to stay hidden when they name an Inn after you. The General Stanton Inn, Charlestown, was named after **Joseph Stanton** (July 19, 1739 - December 15, 1821). He thought he was going to be a military guy. He did well during the Quebec excursion, but he was a better politician. Not only was he a delegate to the Rhode Island Constitutional Convention, he moved up the ladder and served as a United State Senator. In case anybody forgot the story, Rhode Island was the first state to have a chance to adopt the Constitution and said "no." Then we slid back in taking over the 13th slot.

Sometimes when daddy's famous, your name comes up in conversation and everybody thinks they're talking about dad. That's what happened to **William Greene Jr.** (August 16, 1731 - November 29, 1809). His dad was a court clerk and the Speaker of the Assembly who got to be Governor. There was a lot expected of Junior. Not only was daddy

Governor, but grandad served for 10 years as Deputy Governor and great grandad was an original settler of Provide and Warwick. The younger William had every political job you could imagine. Most importantly, when the British showed up, he served on the War Council so the government could still function while we were fighting off the British. Home life was interesting too. I suppose when the young lady you're interested in is pen pals with Benjamin Franklin, you ignore the fact that she's your second cousin and marry her anyway. It all worked out as one of their sons went on to become the Attorney General in South Carolina.

Some folks just get pulled into things. **Henry Marchant** (April 9, 1741 - August 30, 1796) had that happen. He was already a Founding Father, served as Rhode Island Attorney General, was a delegate to the Continental Congress, had signed the Articles of Confederation, and had served as a District Court Judge. He just wanted to have his little private practice in South Kingstown. The Universe said, "No you don't, I'm dragging you to Newport again" to do something else. While that tug of war is happening, George Washington nominates him to serve as a judge on the United States District Court District of Rhode Island. That's how he ends up presiding over West v. Barnes which is the first case ever appealed to the United States Supreme Court.

Sometimes the way somebody was raised explains their behaviors later in life. **Nathanael Greene** (August 7, 1742 - June 19, 1786) had an interesting childhood. His dad was a person to take some Quaker beliefs to the limit. There were eight kids in the family. None were allowed to read, dance, or engage in a lot of stuff the other kids were doing. This annoyed Nathanael to the point where he finally got his dad to hire a tutor so he could study math and law. He just wanted to take over the family business. Then the British ticked him off at an early age and he formed the Kentish Guards, one of the original state militias. By the time he was finished, he was a General, including at Lexington and Concord, who had served with George Washington many times.

Not all Quakers go through the same things. **John Wilbur** (July 17, 1774 - May 1, 1856) learned this the convoluted way. As a Quaker Minister, and more importantly a thinker trying to discover Spiritual design, he thought Spiritual principles were more important than cold acceptance of the Bible. Cold acceptance was becoming increasingly of a British angle. Mr. Wilbur would visit, words would get said, dividing lines would come into play and teams would take sides. It was not before long, and the Religious Society of Friends had once again split again. Amazing all that happened while abortion and/or pedophilia were never issues.

Sometimes those making announcements and speeches get all the play while folks constantly in the background don't get any play at all. I want to make sure that doesn't happen here. **Thomas Tillinghast** (August 21, 1742 - August 26, 1841) was a guy who could put a deal together. He served in the Rhode Island House of Representatives multiple times, got a gig as an Associate Justice with the Supreme Court, and also served on the Council of War. Then he went to serve multiple terms in Congress while making sure his constituents, especially in his hometown of East Greenwich, got what they needed.

Sometimes the deal making was on the quiet side from someone you would never suspect. That was **Gilbert Stuart's** (December 3, 1755 - July 9, 1828) skill. He had been born in Saunderstown and moved to Newport. Found out he could learn more in Scotland about painting and moved there. His friend dies and he moves back. All the while, he's got this idea that he wants to paint George Washington.

When he returns, he starts cutting deals so he can claim the portrait ladder. He did get to do every portrait he ever wanted. Unfortunately, he had a stroke. Stoke plus twelve kids equals no cash late in life. He was buried in Boston in an unmarked grave. There was a plan to change that, but it never came through. If you do get a chance, you need to check out the house and museum in Saunderstown.

Some folks took planning to a new level. **Charles Tillinghas James** (September 15, 1805 - October 17, 1862) did such a great job self-learning mathematics and mechanics that Brown College gave him an honorary Master of Arts Degree in 1838. His specialty was steam mills. Back in those days, small seaport towns knew they wanted a steam mill but that's about all they knew. Mr. James developed a number of successful companies. Along the way, he became a United Senator. He only served one term. Rumors were that he missed that small seaport town cash.

Some folks connected to Brown got to do both. **Henry Bowen Anthony** (April 1, 1815 - September 2, 1884) was a publisher and a politician. At one time he was a co-owner of the Providence Journal. Another time he was Governor. He went on to be President Pro Tem of the United States Senate. Some people were better off when the Legislature made that choice. He did such a fantastic job that he set a record for attendance at his funeral.

It would appear that the crossover between the military and politics affected every occupation. **Job Kenyon** (July 8, 1821 - August 5, 1889) is proof that it was true for physicians as well. During the Civil War, he became the Assistant Surgeon to Rhode Island's 3rd Regiment. After the Civil War, he served in the Rhode Island Senate. He would leave that job later in life to become President of the Rhode Island Medical Society.

Another thing that seems to show up in South County a lot is folks starting on their paths rather early. Without question, **Edward Everett Hale** (April 3, 1822 - June 10, 1909) was a child prodigy. (Yes, in case you're wondering if he was related to Nathan Hale.) After graduating from the Boston Latin School, he enrolled in Harvard College at the ripe old age of thirteen. At the age of twenty, he was already a Unitarian Minister and making waves. In 1959, he started writing with a spiritual bent. He was deeply against slavery and when he became the editor at the Christian Examiner, he had a built-in audience to serve. He would become best known for *The Man Without a Country*.

Sometimes becoming a child prodigy is an unintended circumstance and not a choice. **Thomas Alexander Tefft** (August 2, 1826 - December 12, 1859) grew up with a number of illnesses. That meant he couldn't play outside. Instead, he turned to books. While he was a teenager, **Henry Banard** needed someone who could draw to help him explain the changes in architecture he wanted to suggest. He thought Thomas would be perfect for the job. At 25, Thomas opened his own firm. He worked hard for 5 years and then went on a European tour, where he became ill and died. His body was shipped back to the US a few years later.

Would it surprise you that the "First American Beard of a Political Nature" was from this part of Rhode Island? **Harriet Lane** (May 9, 1830 - July 3, 1903) served that role for James Buchanan. It's time we just deal with the fact that we might have had more than one gay President, the Log Cabin Republicans exist for a reason, in our history. As James Buchanan's niece, Harriet served as Substitute First Lady. The other women in this category all do so after the President's actual wife died. The interesting thing is before magazines and social media, she was an influencer with many women around the country copying her style.

Remember we talked about people who wanted to keep who they were hanging out with a secret? **J. Howard McGrath** (November 28, 1903 - September 2, 1966) fit that one to a tee. He was Attorney General, Governor, US Solicitor General, and US Senator. He was the Democratic National Committee who managed Harry Truman's campaign. He was born in Woonsocket, served in Central Falls, and ran his law office out of Providence. Where was his summer home in which he cut all his deals? Narragansett. Oh my, the stories that driveway could tell.

Joseph Purtill (1927 - March 25, 2014) was born in Westerly. Then he served in the military, moved to Connecticut, and passed the Connecticut Bar. In 1979 he was appointed to the Connecticut Superior Court after serving in the Connecticut House of Representatives. He does not have a "signature case" but go check out the pure number of cases compared to the average. Oh my.

Ruth Buzzi (July 24, 1936) doesn't need an introduction. She was born in Westerly. From 1968-1973, she was a star on Rowan and Martin's laugh track. That experience garnered her a Golden Globe Award and 5 Emmy Nominations.

Since I mentioned TV, this would be a good time to mention **Judge Frank Caprio** (November 24, 1936) is a viral sensation. "Wait a minute Bobby" you ask, "Isn't he all Providence?" Kind of. However, he bought the original Coastguard House restaurant back in 1978. Until he revealed it on Instagram in 2020, a lot of folks didn't know.

Not everybody from South County is as nice as everybody else. **Michael** Woodmansee (July 16, 1958) was 16 years old when he murdered 5-year-old **Jason Foreman** in a neighboring town. If Woodmansee had not tried to kill another child and had gotten questioned during that investigation, he never would have admitted to the first killing. Woodmansee was so emotionally attached to what he did that he kept Foreman's skull and some of his bones in a dresser.

Did you know that **Debra Messing** (August 15, 1968) went to East Greenwich High School? I wonder how many of those references made it into Will and Grace. It should be noted that her son Roman and I share a birthday 37 years apart. She has earned 7 Golden Globe nominations, 5 Emmy Award nominations, and 7 Screen Actors Guild nominations, she scored a win with one of those, in her career.

Ever have that self-conflict where you think a politician stands for things you can't tolerate but at the same time, they do it so well that you can't help but like them? That's how I felt about former **State Representative Ray Sullivan** (January 31, 1977 - October 12, 2021). He grew up in Coventry and went to Roger Williams. While his work as a State Representative was outstanding, his work on campaigns was even better. The one time we were on the same team, I'm a typical Democratic Leadership Council fiscal conservative, was when he was the major force behind getting marriage equality done in Rhode Island. Kids in school who want to be in politics should be taught to read up on his career.

The last entry in this section is a total surprise. **Billy Gilman** (May 24, 1988) was born in Westerly and raised in Hope Valley. If you know a gay young person who is struggling, or one who just wants to be inspired, have them check out the video *My Story* by Billy Gilman. He has done so much beyond the stage to help people.

Next time you're driving in South County, check out the driveways. Take note that when it's an "expensive house," it always curls just a little and there's no markings. Then think about any house on Farewell Street in Newport on an August afternoon. That will help demonstrate the difference between East and West. Just wait a little bit and even the difference is about to become a source of self-conflict for some.

53

Do You Know – South County?

One of the best parts of visiting Rhode Island no matter where you stay is that you're never more than 30 minutes, ok 45 minutes if you decide to visit or leave Newport by the Pell Bridge, from everything else. Therefore everything on this list can be part of your next trip. Some memories are forever.

For instance, you arrive in Rhode Island and decide you want to meet a vampire. You immediately travel over to **the Exeter Historical Cemetery** and pray to the young vampire girls, 100 years apart with the same birthdays, buried there. You might get a chance at the real thing later on.

You might want to pick up something on the way, so stop by the **South County Center for the Arts in South Kingstown**. The styles are always in flux so you're not always looking at the same items over and over again. Prices are moderate considering it's New England art.

Of course you might want to read about the vampires. **The University of Rhode Island** is just a few minutes away. The campus is awe inspiring in its beauty.

One of the things I never forget about South County is while it has remarkable beaches, there are plenty of opportunities to escape into the woods. Tourist areas tend to trend urban. For some people, even the beaches are too crowded yet they want that nature feel. If you're not careful, you can get mentally lost, which is a good thing, and end up in an entirely different part of the state when you get off the trail, which can be time consuming but still fun.

For instance, one of the things you may want to try is the **Potter Memorial Wood**. "The Wood" was originally deeded over to a not-for-profit organization back in 1933 by Mary LeMoine Potter. She literally wanted families to build memories of walking and playing sports and skating. The best part of this experience is when the sun is just right in the sky, it looks like a natural corridor that was meant to be discovered the entire time.

Then again, maybe botanical gardens are more your thing. **The Kinney Azalea Gardens** is one of the best early morning visits you can make. The natural colors are incredibly striking.

If bike paths are more your thing, **Fagan Park** in South Kingstown should definitely be on your list. 1.4 acres of bike riding fun and some of the best engineered stone walls you might see. Best part is water fountains are never far away due to the design.

"Hey Bobby, sounds great but we own a dog. What's in it for us?" you ask. **The Alewife Brook Preserve** is for you. It's a 1-mile loop and not a lot of people know about it so it's usually quiet.

If you decide to stay on the urban side, as you're jumping from place to place you'll notice that manufacturing is the number one industry in South County. I know that's a bit of a surprise. Even more surprising is that healthcare is second, (South County is great to retire to,) and education is third.

Many in Rhode Island would love this to change a little. They wonder why agriculture is always successful in South County but seldom pursued by many. Along those lines, in the spring Rhode Island seniors can sign up to receive a free box of fresh produce provided by local farmers.

The oldest building in Rhode Island is the **Henry Palmer House** in South Kingstown. While it's got an older design, it has a raised ranch feel. Many people immediately think that it would be a cool place to live.

A close second is the **Rocky Meadows Farm House**. If you head over there, see if you can sneak by the neighboring pond especially early in the evening. Something about the sound of frogs calling out to each other so they can make friends on a summer's eve is incredibly calming.

Of course if you're building houses, you need churches to attend. **Old Narragansett Church** is believed to be the oldest Episcopal Church building in the Northeast United States. The wild part is that it was originally built in 1707 a few miles away and moved to its current location a couple of decades after the Revolutionary War.

The 1800's in South County featured constant but quiet growth. That changed a bit in 1848. Joseph Heatly Dulles was on a business trip. Yes, he was the grandfather of the Secretary of State with the same name. On a tour, he became totally enthralled. Next thing anyone knew, summertime trips with family and business associates were a regular tradition.

What started inside the circle became a "we told two friends and so on" deal. Uncle Ezbon Taylor took notice. In 1856, Uncle Ezbon decided that a hotel, the **Narragansett House**, was not only necessary but would be profitable. Not long after that, the Narragansett Pier became a "watering place" for many just trying to get away without being noticed.

For some it's not the feeling or the peace. Some people just like glitz and cash. Even County has one of those. Last time **Sea Grace** in Narragansett was listed, it was for $18 million. The house sits on 2 acres of Ocean road and is easier to see on a boat trip from Martha's Vineyard than it is trying to drive by it.

Some older buildings can't exactly stay the way they were constructed to be. **Kenyon's Department Store** fits that model. Charles Chase and Henry Lewis thought that Wakefield needed a department store back in 1891. The store closed in 1996 and is now part of South County Hospital.

If museums are your thing, the **South County Museum** in Narragansett has to be on the list. Most people tell you the Metz Exhibit Hall makes the trip worth it by itself. My vote would be for the Carpentry Shop.

"Sounds good for us but my kids have been studying the history of Native Americans in class lately. Where should we go?" If seeing Native American artifacts is the goal, the **Tomaquag Museum** is the place to go. Best part of all is it's open year round.

56

If you don't have kids and just want to see early American artifacts, the **South County History Center** is a great way to fill an afternoon. It used to be a jail back in the day so if you get some weird vibes, that's why.

This is not to say that South County is without its silliness. For instance, without mentioning any names or fringe right organizations, somebody in South County files a lot of public records requests. A lot of politicians think my one per week is a lot. This particular person filed 200 of them in one month.

The biggest controversy ever originated in South County was over a hospital parking lot. You should always make sure Native American burial grounds are anywhere near where you plan to put a parking lot. Of course this being Rhode Island, the Native American folks buried there already had neighbors as local governments had been using the spaces as a potter's field for some time.

As always, when you visit anywhere in Rhode Island and especially in South County, bring a change of clothes. You will promise to yourself that you are not going to get dirty or wet. The natural beauty of the surroundings will suck you in.

In fact, Taylor Swift wrote a song called "The Last Great American Dynasty" which tells the story of the previous owner of her Westerly, Rhode Island home, Rebekah West Harkness.

Question: Can you identify this building?
Answer on page 161

All About Block Island

Pictures of Block Island do not do it justice. Why? As beautiful as it is, the feeling of being that far from the rest of the world, you're really not, and at peace is amazing. Then you realize that while you explore the island, no one is going to bother you. This is a big difference between the Island and Newport where street merchants are everywhere.

Dutch explorer Adriaen Block was the second captain to visit the island. Second, because in 1524, Giovanni de Verrazzano saw it first and called it "Claudia." However, he didn't do much after that. I hate to use the word explored because 1.) Columbus never found anything and 2.) Native American folks already canoed over to party away from the rest of the family. In the beginning, it was 16 families from the Massachusetts Colony who relocated there and started the Island's popularity.

By this point, the Narragansetts had already named the Island "Manisses" which translates to "Island of the Little God." Seems the Little God has developed a thing for summertime frolicking. Apparently whenever the Narragansetts visited or entertained, they told other Native Americans about the Island. Wampanoags, Pequots, and Niantics all had settlements there at different times.

It is somewhat funny that Adriaen Block happened on the site. He was supposed to be over in the Hudson. Fur traders had financed his trip thinking he was going to discover access to Upstate New York. Instead,

59

he happened upon the Colonial version of a Native American style Vegas. This is how messed up this whole exploration trope is. In 1636, the Endicott Group showed up and claimed it as theirs even with the Native American folks of different tribes hanging out. Then in 1661, the Group sold it to John Alcock and 15 other people. You can head over to Cow's Cove to see his memorial. In 1672, they became part of the Rhode Island Colony and settled on the name New Shoreham.

The Dutch aren't down with this. As late as 1685, they produced maps calling it Adriaen Block's Island. By the way, if you're having one of those days, looking at old maps has a healing quality.

An interesting thing started to happen in the 1700's. Folks begin to realize that from different spots on the Island, they can see just about everything around them. At that point, they had no idea why that was important. Well until the Revolutionary War showed up.

On April 6, 1776 the Battle of Block Island happened. Six Continental ships couldn't capture the British Fleet's HMS Glasgow. A bunch of folks get fired after that one. I only know that happened because my birthday is the 7th and all through elementary school until I skipped a grade, some teacher had to "do me the favor" of telling me about it.

As you might expect, the biggest known industries on the island are "starting over" and tourism. What you might not expect is that the number one actual industry is kelp farming. This is where I get to remind you that Kelp is technically not a plant.

The population of Block Island is just over 1400. In the summer, that swells to 15,000 in the same space. Paying $30,000 a month for a house rental isn't unheard of. If you're not careful, you might run into Christopher Walken.

The biggest secret about Block Island is the number of psychics who do séances there. Sounds like places where serial killers might have died and Native American massacres happened or good for such exercises. Add in the Ghost Ships that have allegedly docked there and you have yourself a party.

People of Significance – Block Island

Obviously when you choose to live on Block Island, you are isolating a little bit. However, it's not isolation out of anxiety. Usually the goal of isolation is to have better focus on the things that matter to you.

Elizabeth Dickens (December 2, 1877 - June 17, 1963) is a great example of this. You don't get to be called the Bird Lady of Block Island without showing dedication to your craft. She began keeping a daily journal about bird watching, which you can still read if you take a trip up to the Audubon Society in Smithfield. When she wasn't just viewing, she was engaged in taxidermy.

Kenneth Bacon (November 21, 1944 - August 15, 2009) had been a reporter for the Wall Street Journal and a spokesperson for the Department of Defense. He was involved in the first Linda Tripp incident. Later in life, he served as President of Refugees International. Once he got diagnosed with cancer, he spent 90% of his time in his second home on Block Island so he could concentrate on saying goodbye to his family.

Jens Risom (May 8, 1916 - December 9, 2016) was born in Denmark. He came to the United States wanting to be in the furniture business. He ended up getting drafted. When his service ended, he went back to designing furniture. The Rhode Island School of Design thought so much of his work that they made him a trustee. While that was going on he found inspiration for some of his designs on the Island. When he needed to get his head together, that's where he went.

Did you watch a Los Angeles Clippers game right after the "controversy"? **Richard Parsons** (April 4, 1948), have I told you how much I love fellow Aries people with birthdays close to mine?, would have appreciated you. Rumor has it that he was named Interim CEO while on the Island. His life before that was the world. Skipping grades here and there, getting into law school without a degree due to test scores, being a partner in his own firm, his grandfather worked on the Rockefeller Estate so he had all kinds of amazing connections. Unfortunately cancer ended his last gig, CEO of CBS after Les Moonves, earlier than it should have been.

It is always interesting when I am doing one of these and I run into a person I am not a big fan of. Please say "Hello" to Tad Devine (June 11, 1955). Ask Richard Licht and Joe Paolino about our friend. This is not to say he's not incredibly talented. He is. He just makes weird choices all the time. See Paul Manafort - Tad was the first witness at that trial.

We cannot leave this section without mentioning **Christopher Walken** (March 31, 1943). Calling his television, especially Saturday Night Live, and movie career incredible isn't close to doing it justice. The thing is, you have to meet him as I did once in a MacDonald's location that's no longer there back in Newport. My friends who have run into him on Block Island say it's like running into Bill Murray, known for taking fries or sampling drinks off people's trays in the summertime, but with an enticing creepy undertone.

One of the things you will notice about running into a celebrity on Block Island is time moves slower. In Newport, everything is noisy and it's over quickly. On Block Island, time moves at a slower pace and if you're both headed in the same direction, you might get to spend a little time with them. That's what happens when the rest of the world, even though you can see it, seems so far away.

Do You Know – Block Island?

Obviously if you're in your own boat, take as much time as you like getting to Block Island. Whether you should take the high speed or the regular speed ferry comes down to a simple thing. Do you have kids? Kids just wanna get there and love the angle the Ferry motors at. As adults, we want to watch where we disappear slowly knowing we won't have to deal with it for a while. On the way back, we want to hold onto memories as long as possible before dealing with the reality we left behind in the first place.

The best kept secret about Block Island is that if the food being offered looks like it's being prepared in a food truck, it's less expensive and sneaky good. Head over to the Southeast Lighthouse and look around. You'll discover one right next door.

Kind of interesting to think that even with the shoals and ledges just off the coastline, even though the Island was nicknamed the "Stumbling Block" by mariners in the 1800's, the **Southeast Lighthouse** almost didn't get built. There was money appropriated for it twice and the money ended up in other projects and pockets. If Nicholas Ball had not circulated a petition in 1872, it might never have happened.

One of the things you are going to see is continuous maintenance of **Block Island forests**. Back in 2020, a report came out saying all of Rhode Island's forests could be in danger. The folks on Block Island said, "Yeah, no kidding." This too was a matter of advocacy back in the 1800's. Imagine if we had just listened to those people?

It's not like island homeowners cannot spend some money on this effort. The median home listing price right now is $3.2 million. At any given time in the marketplace, about 17-19 homes are available. It should be noted that this is a 214.5% increase since the start of the pandemic.

Once you fork over the down payment and do the paperwork, head over to **Woonsocket House** so you can relax for a little while. Two floors of exhibits to wonder through and put your mind at ease. Even if it's not open in the summer, you can visit via the winter by appointment.

If spirituality is more your thing, you never know - the spirit of Ulysses S. Grant might still be hanging around the **Ocean View Hotel** as this was one of his hideaways. You can head to where the hotel was before it burned to the ground. Some folks claim even walking by it late on a calm summer's night they can hear odd accents saying very old timey things. I find inspiration whenever I'm in the neighborhood.

Block Island is definitely on my "a couple of times" during the summer list. Problem is as I get older, I add more of those places and summer is getting filled. I might just have to make a trip out there in the winter. Weather won't be the same but the healing and spirituality will still be there.

"Small Craft Warnings Block Island to Hatteras.

Whatever that means."

-Breakfast at Tiffany's

All About Blackstone Valley

It never occurs to you until you're leaving Providence. In fact, normally not until you're on the way home. If you had traveled a little further, you would have hit the Blackstone Valley. There are plenty of places there that you have always wanted to try.

That whole tucked in Northeastern portion of the state starting just north of Providence and running all the way to Worcester is something to behold. 263,000 people are proud to call the Valley home on the Rhode Island side.

The best part about the Valley is it does not matter what you are into. If early technology is your thing, Slater Mill is here. If a long walk through the trees is more of what you need, just make a trip over to Lincoln Woods.

Originally the Valley was inhabited by the Narragansetts, Wampanoags, and Nipmucs. In 1635, Reverend Blackstone brought a congregation to hunt and explore. A year later, Roger Williams shows up in Providence. As things always go, some folks don't get along and settle into the woods a little further North.

Both sides got along until 1675 when King Philip's War happened. At that point it was pretty much over for the Native American population. The moment they could get their hands on more land, settlers wanted to fill it with elements spawned off the Industrial Revolution.

In the beginning, it was mill, mill, and mill. If water ran somewhere, you put a mill next to it so wheels could spin and cotton could be turned into items you could sell. Little did those folks know that some of their properties would become prime office space 300 years later.

That in turn has led to other surprises. For instance, most folks do not know that Cumberland is the unofficial ice cream capital of the Blackstone Valley. You might also be surprised to discover that the #1 spot to take a selfie north of Providence is in Woonsocket. Bronze statues will do that.

So for the next little bit, forget how much time we need to get back. Let's adventure a little but to the north to see what's waiting for you. I promise it will be worth it.

People of Significance – Blackstone Valley

I always when I get to the "people" section. I offer an apology. Some of your favorites most likely didn't make it. However, there were some flavors I didn't even know existed in Blackstone Valley that I just had to highlight. I hope you can forgive me.

Starting with people I didn't even know were from Blackstone Valley, let us start with Public Universal Friend (November 29, 1752 - July 1, 1819). They started life in Cumberland as Jemima Wilkinson. Jemima thought after suffering a severe illness in 1776 that they died and were reincarnated. Then they went on and preached with **the Universal Friends**. Think Quakers lite designed to attract women.

He's not the only person who did some change or realization. **Samuel Slater** (June 9, 1768 - April 21, 1835) was the Father of the Industrial Revolution in the United States. In England, he was known as Same the Slate due to the number of times he bought British technology, brought it to the United States, made a few adjustments, and then rebranded it as American. By the time he's done, he's going to own 13 mills.

He will also be responsible for creating company towns like Slatersville because his mills inspired John Slater (December 25, 1776 - May 27, 1843), Samuel's younger brother, to have the idea. He wasn't trying to change the way we lived when he helped design a building that had the owner's house, homes for workers, and the company store all on the same site but he sure did. Like his brother, he was greatly influenced by what he saw in England.

Someone had to put these buildings together. That's where **David Wilkinson** (January 5, 1771 - February 3, 1852) came in. He was trained as a mechanical engineer. While his building contributions are a big deal, it is more important that he invented a lathe for cutting screw threads.

Some of the folks who worked in mill like environments had amazing kids. **Isabelle Ahearn O'Neil** (1880 - 1975) was 1 of 13 kids. She would go on to become Rhode Island's first woman elected to the Rhode Island Legislature. Somehow the family set it up so that while she was being educated at the Boston College of Drama and Oratory, she was taking physical education classes over at Harvard. That would lead to an amazing silent film career.

Thankfully, in one way, textile firms were not good at disposing of textile remains. Herman, Hillel, and Henry Hassenfeld were incredibly appreciative. Oh that's right, you know them as **Hasbro**. GI Joe? Hasbro. Parker Brothers? Hasbro. While the Hassenfeld brothers didn't know about Peppa Pig, she belongs to their company now.

Sometimes it's not what you play with but what you listen to. David Olney (March 23, 1948 - January 18, 2020) recorded over 20 albums in his life. His albums have been covered by Linda Ronstadt and Steve Earle. While he was born in Providence, according to friends, he did a lot of his early writing on trips through the **Blackstone Valley**.

Vice Admiral Walter E. Carter Junior (Nov 4, 1959) is a native of Burrillville. He became a Naval Flight Officer in 1982. In 2013, he became the President of the Naval War College.

Aaron Fricke (January 25, 1962) was born in Pawtucket. He is the Fricke in Fricke v. Lynch. That case allowed same sex partners to attend a prom for the first time. Now he spends his time as an activist and writer.

Viola Davis (August 11, 1965) attended Rhode Island College. Her acting career started in Central Falls. Amazing that an off-off Broadway star can lead to an Emmy, a Grammy, an Oscar, and a Tony. Her career continues to be amazing, in 2009 she was inducted into the Academy of Motion Picture Arts and Sciences, whether she acts or produces on stage or screen.

A promised you a little different flavor. **Nap Lajoie** (September 5, 1874 - February 7, 1959) is a **Blackstone Valley** guy. I've been to his plaque in the Hall of Fame. I know about the 20-year career and the rivalry with Ty Cobb. I had no idea that he was born in Woonsocket.

One can only wonder what **Don Orsillo** (December 16, 1968) calling play by play for one of his games would have sounded like. Don Orsillo's career is coming up on 30 years if you count his time with the Pawtucket Red Sox. Even though he has moved around a little, he has always kept ties from that era.

Sometimes we forget that **Gina Raimondo** (May 17, 1971) had an impressive venture capitalist career before she started the amazing political career she has now. Not everybody gets to be Governor and then United States Secretary of Commerce. Even fewer folks graduate magna cum laude from Harvard and end up in a firm backed by Bain Capital.

Lincoln, Rhode Island is also the birthplace of a New York Times bestselling author who specializes in young adult and romance novels. **Sarah MacLean** (December 23, 1978) had a dream as a teenager that writing is what she wanted to do, and she pulled it off. Folks noticed her early talents back when she was attending Smith College.

I bet you didn't know the Blackstone Valley had a Venn Diagram like gay rights and sports crossover? Anybody who had voted in Rhode Island a couple of times never would have guessed that. All you have to do to experience it is driving a little past Providence from the South or schedule a little time to stop on the way in from the North.

Do You Know – Blackstone Valley?

Whenever you travel to Rhode Island but especially true in the Blackstone Valley area, take a pause and visit some mills. 90% of the time, mills are next to water. Just the way the mill fits into the landscape can be a beautiful sight. In Northern Rhode Island, this is doubly true.

When you get done visiting the mills, you're going to be hungry. Go over to North Smithfield and visit **Wright's Dairy Farm**. The bakery might actually be tastier than any of the dairy products. Ssshhhhhh don't tell anybody.

For some people food isn't what makes them feel better. Would young people achieving what they've been told their whole lives is beyond their reach do it for you? Stop by **Central Falls High School** and ask about the branch of the Upward Bound program located there. Yes, the first story will be about Viola Davis but there will be many more to share.

If reaching the previously unobtainable does it for you, **Frank Lloyd Wright** grew up in Pawtucket on Blackstone Avenue. If you stop by number 12, please keep in mind that according to some people, ummm, he's still there. Amazing with all the buildings he designed all over the country that he would choose to haunt his boyhood home, but people like what they like.

Those aren't the only ghosts you can visit. Supposedly nighttime at the Cumberland Library is its own show. This is what happens when you turn a monastery into a library. Some folks just don't want to let go.

There is one more spot to check out. Sometimes it's not about holding on. Sometimes it's about knowing something won't exist soon. **The Apex Building** in Pawtucket fits that bill. Supposedly since the sale to the city in 2021, eerie things have been happening as some spirits are not happy. Maybe it is the pyramid shape that gives the location this power.

That might be a little too ghosty for some folks. If you want to take a breath, **Blackstone River State Park** is a short drive away. Of course if you try to swim in the Blackstone River at the moment, you might join the ghosts.

Yes, the Blackstone Valley is much more spiritual than you thought. I think that is due to the struggles folks growing up in the region had to overcome to achieve their desired success. Tough childhoods apparently can hang on right into the afterlife.

"Rhode Island is famous for you, little state, you know what to do, freezing tongues and noses, doorbells ring, Icicles cling, very nice to be, quarantined with you." –
Neil Sedaka, Singer and Songwriter

All About Greater Providence

Welcome to Greater Providence. Outside of cities that have welcomed numerous refugee populations, see Utica, New York, it is hard to imagine a municipal area being more culturally diverse. That also enhances the food at every level.

For purposes of this section, we're looking at Providence, East Providence, North Providence, and Johnston. While being one of the most Italian and Catholic sections of the country carries part of the story, it is not the whole tale. 300,000 people with common ties can drive a lot statewide.

Because certain new channels exist that don't exactly care about truth, you may have been told that cities are not safe. The reality is that per capita, you are 50% safer in a big city. Providence carries this trend forward being one of the safer cities again per capita. It should also be noted that if you have kids and are looking for a private school for them to attend, you've got some great choices.

The foundation in Greater Providence's economy is food. However, in the last few years, high tech has taken off. This is especially true for life sciences based on technology and IT software. Data Analytics are not far behind.

As is true with many places in Rhode Island, water plays a big role. Providence sits at the top of the bay and water winds its way through the city creating many landscape design opportunities. Just walk from downtown up to the college section.

Roger Williams gets tossed out of the Massachusetts Bay Colony in 1636 and arrives in Providence hoping to establish a place where "liberty of conscience was available. He established the first Baptist Church in America in 1638. Because he got to Providence first, he will attract many like him.

In 1660, **King Charles II** came back to rule England. This sets up a number of ripple effects for all of what will be Rhode Island. In Providence, many progressive laws were suddenly ignored. **The Colony of Rhode Island and Providence Plantations** was incredibly progressive for the time abolishing witchcraft trials, the death penalty, and debt imprisonment. They even passed an anti-slavery law 8 years earlier. Once the King returned, many progressive reforms started to be ignored in order to incur favor with him.

The War of 1812 hit Rhode Island differently than other states. Due to the influence of Providence, the state of Rhode Island almost succeeded. As the War was closing, **The Committee of Defence** was created and they went around building militia like fortifications in fear they were going to go through the whole thing all over again. Because the times were the times, while the War ended in February 1815, some folks did not know until after the summer was over.

If history like this intrigues you, **The Roger Williams Park Museum of Natural History and Planetarium** is a great place to reach deeper understanding. Exhibits, education and research are all on display. The Park itself has been around since 1871 and grows as Rhode Island grows.

The 19th century was a wild time to live in Providence. While the mills were doing the work up in the **Blackstone Valley**, the design enhancements were created in Providence. The Industrial Revolution also meant that economies had to be managed entirely differently. A lot of that trial and error went on in Providence.

That is also going to create some weird spinoffs. A great economy means you get to have a heavy influence in sports since your community can support a team. Can you name the last defunct NFL team to win a title? That would be the **Providence Steam Roller** in 1928. In those days, you won the title by achieving the best winning percentage which was important since the Frankfort franchise actually won 3 more games.

As you walk through the history of the region, you begin to realize that pictures add to the story better than words do. This is especially true for the 1940's and 1950's in Greater Providence. There's that view of life that looks like it came straight off a television program from the era. In most places, this exchange is full of falsehoods. In Providence it is totally true.

A lot of this is due to the power the Providence Mayor has. Spoiler alert - there is more than one of them in the "People of" section. Around the state, many folks have an easier time naming the Mayor of Providence than they do their own State Representative or State Senator.

If you visit Providence, the first thing you will notice is **Amica Mutual Pavillion.** Most people still call it The Dunk. Elder folks never stopped calling it the **Civic Center**. For most Rhode Islanders, it was the site of their first concert experience in high school or college.

This is not to say that **Greater Providence** is not without its challenges. Because it is New England, profit is even more of a concern, especially for drug dealers. We all thought Fentanyl had changed the game. Now, Fentanyl is getting cut with another substance and those recipes are showing up in Providence first. As a member of the **Recovery Community**, I will spend even more time 12 stepping in the alley ways off **Kennedy Plaza** where all the bus lines still come together.

Once again, we now live in a sad world where some political groups try to make cities sound as if they are inhabitable. While there are problems, cities pay the bills, are responsible for most of the entertainment, and always lead in innovation. **Greater Providence** does much more than its share in those categories.

People of Significance – Greater Providence

One thing you will notice as we talk about the amazing people of Greater Providence is that some of them have a hard time following the law. Some of them do it secretly, some of them do it brazenly

In the spring of 1637, **William Carpenter** (1610 - September 7, 1665) showed up in Providence Plantations. While he's here, he'll end up serving in just about every office imaginable. Need a Town Councilor? See William. Want to get married and need a Justice of the Peace? See William. Need a Town Meeting Moderator? See William.

John Brown (January 27, 1736 - September 20, 1803) was a merchant and a slave trader who didn't like the way banks did business so he founded his own. He became President of Providence Bank in 1791. Because the major abolitionist of the next era was also named John Brown, you can imagine some of the conversations in the early 1800's. The Rhode Island John Brown went from being an agitator at the Gaspee Incident to being a co-founder of the College of Rhode Island which became Brown University.

Paulina Kellogg Wright Davis (August 7, 1813 - August 24, 1876) came to Rhode Island for love. She actually was born in New York and her first marriage was in Utica, one of my favorite cities ever. She had already started helping women learn about science and medicine. After her first husband's death, she falls in love with Thomas Davis, a Democrat from Rhode Island, and gets married in Providence. This is where her suffragist career begins.

Henry Lippitt (October 9, 1818 - June 5, 1891) is one of the first people to make the move from big business to politics. He owned some fantastic mills including the Hanora and Social Mills in Woonsocket while also serving as a bank Vice President. That wasn't good enough as he also wanted to be Governor.

Some folks get their start in vaudeville instead of big business. I wish vaudeville was around when I was a kid. **George M. Cohen** (July

74

3, 1878 - November 5, 1942) wrote more than 50 shows and produced over 300 songs in his career. If you ever find yourself singing Over There or Give My Regards to Broadway or You're a Grand Old Flag you can thank him.

John Chaffee (October 22, 1922 - October 24, 1999) owes some of his political success to the Lippitt family. Henry Lipitt was his great grandfather. After serving in the Marines, he went from the Rhode Island General Assembly to the Governor's Office. He would then serve in the US Senate proving that the Southern Strategy was real, being one of the last Pro Choice Republicans. His son would follow the same path.

Some folks have no intention of moving here but experiencing the nighttime, not necessarily the nightlife but the beauty of Rhode Island in the nighttime, hooks them. That's what happened to Alan Shawn Feinstein (1931). He was teaching part-time when not writing shoe advertisements. The young psychiatrist he was dating fell in love with the Cranston night sky. When they got married, they moved here. Somehow, writing books and collecting baseball cards worked for him. He is incredibly charitable but he has this need to have his name on things which sometimes causes issues.

One thing I have learned is it is always the internal issues that cause the problems. Blaming things on "greed" or someone being "power hungry" is way too simplistic. Such was the case for **Mayor Vincent "Buddy" Cianci** (April 30, 1941 - January 28, 2016). He was an incredible mayor, better than average talk show host, but best of all, good human. Unfortunate, sexual insecurities drove him to do some things that got him in trouble. He was always sleeping with somebody but his need to protect turf took over. That was also true for his grift. While he liked the limousine, his lifestyle could have been way more lavish than it was. He needed the money, he thought, to attract the women.

A lot of folks forget that before **Ernie Digregorio** (January 15, 1951) led Providence College, he had already taken North Providence High to a Class B State Championship. He did take the Friars to the 1973 Final 4. After that he had a 5 year NBA career closing out with the Celtics.

Meredith Vieira (December 30, 1953) shares a lot with my family because her family comes from the Azores. Raised in East Providence, she attended the Lincoln School and then Tufts University. Her career started in Massachusetts radio and then as a local television reporter. Hard work took her to New York City. A bit of luck causes her to land over kin Chicago showing her skills. Before she gets done, she will have been on *60 Minutes*, hosted the *CBS Morning News*, was the original moderator of *The View*, hosted *Who Wants to Be a Millionaire?* and was a co-host on *Today*.

Some folks make lists because they do really offensive things that are also incredibly intellectually insulting. **Former State Senator and Johnston Mayor Joseph Polisena** (June 27, 1954) makes the list for those reasons. When he was a State Senator, even though he was a Democrat, he once brought a fake fetus to the Rhode Island Senate Floor in an attempt to deny women their rights.

Joe Paolino (April 26, 1955) is my favorite Providence mayor of all time. It helps that he was a local chair of the 1992 Clinton campaign when I was chosen to be Field Coordinator for the \primaries. That decision was made in the Superman Building. Yes, there are some things he's doing today that I find troubling. Those would be trying to purchase a Christopher Columbus Statue and attempting to break up Kennedy Plaza without concern for how it will affect the mentally ill and addicted communities. However, when you know somebody comes from an honest space, you can openly disagree with them but still like them. We've lost a lot of that as a society.

Some folks need to have their careers looked at "en toto" to see the true impact. That would be true for fellow Aries Michael Corrente (April 6, 1959). If you get a chance, go watch Federal Hill which won the Audience Award at the Deauville Film Festival back in 1994.

Could we get through this section without mentioning somebody connected to MTV? Of course not. **Paul Delvecchio** (July 5, 1980) first introduced himself as Pauly D on Jersey Shore. Living in Providence, where he was born, he was actually hired off of Myspace.

Do You Know – Greater Providence?

Not everybody is a hero but if their heart is in the right place, they can still be meaningful. Literally no one on this list is without fault. In the cases of all but one, they did cool things. Forgiveness, and realizing none of us are perfect, is a virtue.

One thing that makes Rhode Island different is that there's no County Government. Every "big" political project has to run through Providence. I didn't truly appreciate the difference until I moved to Utica, New York in the Upstate region. One day, I had something that needed "an approval". I thought I had to plan a trip to Albany, which is a 2- hour ride. "Bobby, just head down to the County Building, no problem." The constant ping ponging in and out of Providence means there's some Providence residue all over the state.

Did you know North Providence had its own beach? **Twin Rivers Beach East** sits on the Wenscott Reservoir. The beach is a big favorite of truly outdoor types since there is a campground right next door.

Along those lines, most folks do not know, even folks who live literally minutes away, I would be one of those people, that East Providence has a lighthouse. **Pomham Rocks Lighthouse**, built in 1871, sits nicely over the Providence River. The feature everyone talks about is the 40 foot octagonal tower.

The connection to nearby water has definitely influenced the **Rhode Island School of Design Art Museum**. This is especially true in the 18th and 19th century galleries. John Goddard's work illustrates this very nicely.

One of the nice things about a "water influence" is it does not always have to be the beauty that provides the entertainment. Providence actually has its own swamp. **The Forestack Meadow Swamp** hides over by the river. The whole area attracts creatures that talk to each other because even when you build over things, the creatures don't forget.

Back in the 1730's or so, a lot of the water had not been built over. We forget that sometimes older art was influenced by things we can no longer see. The works of Katherine Holden and Eliza Barnes Weeden are great examples of that principle. If lost inspiration excites you, make a visit to the John Brown House.

Because Rhode Island was somewhat off a mess governance wise from 1650 until 1812, another water influenced concept was Piracy. Everywhere else this was thought as evil. In Rhode Island, it was the third ranking industry. At the time, the Rhode Island government was so cool with the pirates that they charged them a "vig." Now I need to find out what the pirate term for vig was.

Many of these transactions took place on **Gingerbread Island** and **Pancake Island**. Makes you wonder if kids going to school in East Providence would have their imaginations ignited if they knew pirates used to visit those island spots they can barely see from the bus. Then again, that might cause them to ask what a "vig" is.

The first **Washington Bridge** over the Seekonk River between Providence and East Providence was designed as a drawbridge. It has been replaced many times. The 1930 version was converted into the walkable and bikeable **George Redman Linear Park**. Yes, you can see the islands from there as well.

Sooner or later, nighttime is going to hit. Looking for islands, especially in fall and winter, won't be as entertaining. I suggest dinner and a movie. Being that you're in Providence, I'm going to suggest Quahogs. Having been adopted by a Portuguese family, I'm going to suggest Stuffed Quahogs with Chourico as part of the stuffing.

For the movie, especially if you just came off the trail and are on the east side of Providence, I'm going to say the **Avon Cinema** which has been open since 1938. Just the Art Deco architecture makes it worthwhile.

Then you should drive up to **Federal Hill** and just take a walk. If you weren't on the East Side, picking a restaurant on The Hill is a never miss. While I'm no fan of Columbus, you cannot blame Italian folks for celebrating their own heritage and family memories. Until you do Columbus Day on The Hill, Utica is a close second, you really haven't done a proper celebration.

If it's Sunday morning and church going is your thing, there are plenty of choices. No, I'm not a Baptist. Yes, Baptists in other parts of the country are sometimes doing some things we wish they wouldn't. None of that should stop you from visiting **The First Baptist Church in America**. It is one of those houses of worship that carries great emotional residue.

All of Greater Providence is pretty walkable. Before Uber and Lyft, this was sometimes a problem because you'd get mentally lost and end up 5 or 6 miles away from where you started from. In the modern era it is a minor inconvenience.

Question: Where is the International Tennis Hall of Fame located?
Answer on page 161

"Rhode Island is neither a road nor an island.
Discuss."
Bill Bryson, Author and Journalist

Photo credit: Filetime

Question 1: Can you identify this photo?
Answer on page 161

Photo credit: Decontini

Questions 2 & 3: Can you identify these photos?
Answers on page 161

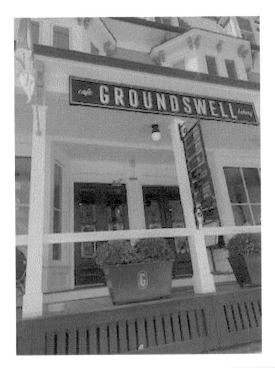

Questions 4 & 5: Can you identify these photos?
Answers on page 161

Questions 6 & 7: Can you identify these photos?
Answers on page 161

Question 8: Can you identify this building?
Answer on page 161

Question 9: Can you identify this neighborhood?
Answer on page 161

85

Question 10: What is this building?
Answer on page 161

Question 11: What are the two buildings in this photo?
Answer on page 161

Question 12: This is the Allendale Mill. Where is it located?
Answer on page 162

Question 13: Where is this island located?
Answer on page 162

87

Question 14: Can you identify this photo?
Answer on page 162

Question 15: Where is this post office located?
Answer on page 162

Question 16: Can you identify this photo?
Answer on page 162

Question 17: Can you identify this bridge?
Answer on page 162

Question 18: Where is this gazebo located?
Answer on page 162

All About Warwick,
West Warwick & Cranston

In 2019, my wife, then girlfriend, and I decided I would leave Utica and move back to Rhode Island so we could live together instead of seeing each other when someone wanted to drive 6 hours or jump on a train. I had grown up in Tiverton, Fall River and Newport. In college, I had even dated a young lady from Cranston. I thought Warwick was all suburban life and industrial parks. Oh My God was I wrong. I've lived here for just over 3 years and 1 week doesn't go by when I don't discover something new and beautiful. Turns out that's true for West Warwick and Cranston as well.

In case you're wondering, I used to live on Bellevue Avenue with a jacuzzi when my wife and I first started dating. Why leave the island at all? Of course I didn't know how cool Warwick was.

Let me go out of turn and start with the thing most locals would like me to say. The airport, Rhode Island T. F. Green International Airport, is here in Warwick. It is literally a 1 mile walk from where I am typing this. There is no airport in Providence. When you fly in, you'll fly here and be right next to all the places I am about to discuss.

I have a lot of personal history with the airport because I spent a great deal of my childhood there. When my father, an electrical engineer, was on the design teams for the SUBROC and Tomahawk missiles, I was constantly at the airport as a young kid saying goodbye or welcoming him back. One of his big destinations was Akron, Ohio. I had no idea what a big role Akron would play in my life but it has.

Speaking of family relations, there's still a fight over whether Cranston is named Samuel Cranston, the longest serving Rhode Island Governor, or Thomas Cranston, the Rhode Island Speaker at the time. Technically, the name emerges from the Scottish. It means "settlement of cranes."

Three industries are always vying for and flip flopping over the lead for the number 1 industry here in Kent County. Right now, it's healthcare followed by retail and manufacturing. However, if the economy re-bounds to pre-pandemic levels, retail might surge again.

West Warwick knows how fast it can change. At the start of the 19th Century, it was all about farming. Then the Industrial Revolution happened. If you check a map, you can see all the waterways in West Warwick. Suddenly mills were being built next to them. I cannot say this enough - if you want to see amazing views of water in a new light, walk through some of the mill areas.

One of the weird things about Warwick and the surrounding areas is while plenty of celebrities live here, (a low crime rate plus high property values will do that,) the communities are home to literally hundreds of celebrity look-alikes. If you "rent" a look alike, more than likely they live here. This can cause interesting exchanges in grocery stores and at the local mall.

The biggest tourist site used to be Rocky Point Park. The amusements are gone but the property is still set aside for walking. As in many spots on the water in Warwick, the views are amazing.

If you drive down to the park, you're only 15 or 20 minutes away, depending on the traffic, from Pawtuxet Village. That's where Cranston and Warwick come together on the water. Starting with the ice cream, the food is outstanding. The Narragansetts named the area which means "Little Falls."

Would you like to hit the best beach with the least crowds? Head down to Conimicut Point. It does not get busy until after 3 pm and it is pet friendly. Barrington across the way looks amazing.

One of the reasons we can't go far back in history with West Warwick is because it was only incorporated in 1913. At the time, Democrats wanted to control the textile center and leave the farmlands to the east to the Republican deals. Political deals like this happen all the time and then history tries to cover them up.

Would you like to hit the best beach with the least crowds? Head down to Conimicut Point Beach. It does not get busy until after 3 pm and it is pet friendly. Barrington across the way looks amazing. I would know because when I first moved here, I jogged there daily.

As is always the case, I will try to point out the less visited, less obvious places to visit. That's the real way to build memories. This is especially true when there are so many great choices.

People of Significance - Warwick, West Warwick & Cranston

There is a way that Warwick is different from Cranston and West Warwick that stands out. Warwick lives with a constant conundrum the other communities do not. Warwick does not want to become "tourist dependent" like Newport is. At the same time, everyone in Warwick wishes their small businesses just had 2 or 3 more customers every weekend. Trying to find "just right" can be a difficult task. Cranston and West Warwick would deal with the traffic and the noise happily.

If you are a gentleman reading this, what underwear are you wearing right now? Did **Benjamin Knight** (October 3, 1813 - June 4, 1898) design it, along with his brother and partner Robert Knight, by any chance? Now you know how Fruit of the Loom happened. The Knights were born in Cranston.

Sometimes it is good to be the last person to do "x" in a state's history; sometimes it's not so good. For **John Gordon** (1815 - February 14, 1845) it wasn't good. Not only was the case filled with shaky circumstantial evidence and anti-Irish Catholic bias that caused him to die by hanging, the state decided to posthumously pardon him in 2011.

Some scientists like germs, some scientists like crabs. For **Dorothy Bliss** (February 13, 1916 - December 26, 1987) land crabs were specifically her thing. She is considered to be a pioneer in the field of crustacean hormonal control. Her peers thought so much of her that she served as the President of the American Society of Zoologists.

MacGyver, Entertainment Tonight, and America's Funniest Home Videos all have one person in common. That would be producer **Vin Di Bona** (April 10, 1944). The Cranston native actually got his reality television start with Battle of the Network Stars.

The next name I am going to bring up is going to cause some folks some stress. I ask you to separate artists from their devotion to a certain politician. If you walk into the average "thrift shop" in Warwick, you will see a picture of **James Woods** (April 18, 1947). He does have 3 Emmys, 3 Screen Actors Guild Awards, two Academy Award nominations and a Golden Globe. He gets it enough that he does his own voice on Family Guy and The Simpsons.

Sometimes it's nice when somebody beats all the expectations. When **Frank Picozzi** (June 21, 1959) decided to run for mayor of Warwick, everybody knew about his great Christmas light displays. They were also worried that he was trying to be a Trump-like populist. Turns out he is a very popular mayor who folks on both sides agree with most of the time. Even more importantly, you get the feeling that no matter what he's working on, it's from the heart. He also has a very hands-on approach to everything including city maintenance which you don't observe from just about all other Rhode Island politicians.

I didn't think I was going to get to list a current Presidential candidate in this list but as it turns out, I do. Former Cranston Mayor **Steve Laffey** (1962) announced his intentions to run for the highest office in the land in 2024. When he was mayor, he was a mini-Trump populist without the racist angle. He had his moments, but like others who get caught up in populism they were overshadowed by silliness.

Vinny Paz (December 16, 1962) knows a little bit about silliness. His path to the lightweight and junior middleweight championships were amazing. Not even a broken neck due to a car accident could keep him from winning. After he quit boxing in 2004, leaving the game with a 50-10 record, his addictions caught up to him. For Paz, he officially changed it from Pazienza in 2001, it started with Blackjack. We just hope he can find strength in recovery.

Few candidates for Texas Governor are born in Rhode Island. **Wendy Davis** (May 16, 1963), born in West Warwick, is the exception to the rule. Her biggest claim to fame was leading the filibuster on an anti-choice bill in the Texas Senate in 2013.

Boardwalk Empire, Game of Thrones, True Blood, and Marco Polo all have something in common. That would be Warwick-born Director **David Petraca** (November 10, 1965). Amazingly for the millennial crowd, he also directed 7 episodes of Dawson's Creek.

Believe it or not, The View does have conservative hosts from time to time. One of them was from Cranston. **Elisabeth Hassellbeck** (May 28, 1977) actually started her career on Survivor: The Australian Outback.

What do you mean there's a Ms. Universe from Rhode Island? I mean **Olivia Culpo** (May 8, 1992) is from Cranston. Are you noticing a pattern? To say the least, she is a social media influencer.

I will only mention this real quickly for a moment since I'm doing a longer segment on it later. **Nicholas O'Neill** (January 28, 1985 - February 20, 2003) was the youngest person to die in the Station Nightclub Fire. I pray for him and the other victims, which will make more sense in a little bit, daily.

Rhode Island has a great tradition of religious freedom. That includes freedom from religion. **Jessica Ahlquist** (June 21, 1995) not only talked the talk but walked the walk. She was the Plaintiff in Ahlquist v.

Cranston that removed a religious prayer from a high school auditorium. To say the least, she put up with a lot of harassment.

I bet you didn't guess how Cranston heavy this list was going to be. That's what happens when one side is trying to stay quiet but successful and the other side just wants attention and will take everything else in trade. If some Cranston folks lived in Newport for a full summer, I wonder if they'd continue to go down that road?

Do You Know - Warwick, West Warwick & Cranston?

You will find that folks who may not live in this part of the state still have intense emotional bonds with certain locations in this part of the state. We are going to go over a few of those. If it makes you uncomfortable, well, that's the point.

We start with the Station Nightclub Fire. On February 20, 2003, Great White was supposed to play at that location. Just before the band started, their manager set off pyrotechnics. The sparks ignited foam soundproofing that covered the walls and ceiling. A human stampede for the exits began. By the time it was over, 100 people were dead.

Here in Rhode Island, a large number of us were supposed to go that night and didn't. In my case, I was coming up on 5 months clean and sober. On that day, I was supposed to go. Around the middle of the afternoon, I started to get iffy. I would get calls and start backing out. I ended up not going. I still do not know what moved me not to go.

Warwick was colonized in 1642. Native American scholars might suggest it was illegally sold by someone who had no right to in exchange for an amount of wampum that was less than what was promised. Whether Samuel Gorton did the cheating or Miantonomi did the cheating, it sure seems like there was cheating. That would be followed by a couple of revolts and a raid. Looking back, that sounds very Rhode Island.

It is amazing that folks so caught up in their own need for corruption could build such amazing Lighthouses. The Warwick Lighthouse is a testament to this conundrum. It was built in Warwick Neck in 1827 and you can still visit it.

However, you have to go a little further north if you want to see where the HMS Gaspee got torched. Its job was to enforce the Navigation Acts. One day it ran aground while chasing another vessel. Abraham Whipple and John Brown who hated the British, not to mention thinking they were funny, lit it on fire. It is considered to be the first act of the Revolution before it would truly start a few years later. The parade every year is pretty impressive.

If after the parade you hang around until Tuesday, you can check out the West Warwick Farmers Market. It runs July through October outdoor patio style. Everything featured is locally grown.

Maybe you're more in the mood to hit things instead of buying them. In that case, head over to the Cranston Country Club. It was developed in the late 60's. When's the last time you hit an approach shot onto an island green?

When you get done with the round of golf, you can take a trip over to Operation Made. They help Veteran -owned and military product-based companies sell their products. The best part is everything is made in the USA.

As is always the case in Rhode Island, if those activities aren't your thing but ghosts are, there is something for you to enjoy. The Sprague Mansion is home to the Cranston Historical Society and some ghosts that have no interest in leaving. It was built back in 1790.

Perhaps you're not in the mood for anything but a sugar coma. You could visit the Lady Ann Candies' Candyland Market. There is no way to describe this and do it justice. It has to be seen. I apologize if you have tooth problems already since this will not help.

You might be desiring performing arts at a much less than usual performing arts cost. I would then suggest the Arctic Playhouse. The building started out as a department store.

In each one of these examples, I can guarantee that someone, or many someones, has built an emotional attachment to them. You can feel it when you walk in the building. Even if you leave with your pockets empty, you usually carry something away in your heart.

Did you know? Rhode Island's State House was completed in 1904 and boasts one of the largest self-supported marble domes in the world.

John Pastore, the first Italian-American to serve as a governor or member of the U.S. Senate, was a dominant figure in Rhode Island politics for three decades. He was an eloquent and highly respected force on Capitol Hill while serving in the Senate.

Foster Glocester

Need a spot that features trout fishing, 10 miles of trails, pond swimming in the summer and cross-country skiing in the winter? **Pulaski State Park** offers that and more. For those of you who drive electric vehicles, I rented a Tesla on my 2- week honeymoon in 2022 and it was awesome, the park also features a charging station.

When you get done, visit **Cady's Tavern.** The drinks are great and all but for the real fun, you need to get there right after closing or right before opening. Let's just see that the beer mugs don't always stay still and the jukebox might have a playlist of its own it likes to listen to.

Not all spirits happen because of humans. **Little Bett** the elephant was just crossing a bridge on the way to do a show when she got gunned down. Supposedly if you visit the plaque late enough at night, you can hear her say hello to the world from beyond.

Perhaps showing your respects to animals is your thing. The **Harmony Ceremony and Chapel Association** has something just for you. **Colonel Chico** is buried there. The Colonel is not a human Colonel. No, it's a former pet monkey. Apparently this was somewhat advertised at the time. You can imagine the commotion that caused.

Do you like doing things with a greater chance of success in your favor? If that's true and the activity is fishing, you should try out **Gorham Farm Pond**. Locals will tell you that in the pond, hot dogs might be the best form of bait.

Maybe you're not all about fishing. Maybe history is more your thing? Did you hear what you could find at **Bowdish Reservoir**? Wander around and you'll stumble into an unmarked Native American grave or two. Unfortunately, being unmarked nothing is known about them except for the Native American part due to the style.

Would you like to visit the oldest continuously operating general store in the entire country? **The Brown and Hopkins Store**, opened in 1799, is waiting for you. Actually started as a hattery and turned into a general store along the way. Today, it features penny candy, antiques, gourmet food, a bakery, and a cafe.

As you can see, there's plenty of reasons to spend the night most folks don't know about. Sadly, there aren't a lot of places to stay that aren't over in Warwick or Providence. Maybe you can change that.

People of Significance - Foster Glocester

When I was a kid, **Salty Brine** was the most dominant radio personality of the day. That's why we all know the mantra "No School Foster Glocester." Therefore, there had to be a Foster Glocester section. The first time I met **Salty** was in the men's room of the **Olde Grist Mill in** Seekonk. At the age of 12, I didn't think famous people went to the bathroom, never mind show up in the one I was in. He was way cool.

The Narragansetts referred to this area as **West Quanaug**. **William Vaughn**, **Zacariah Rhodes**, and **Robert Wescott** originally purchased the real estate. New settlers who were unhappy with the way things were going in Newport immediately made the trip north. Legal process wise, Foster itself was originally part of Scituate until 1781.

That's not all it attracted. In the 1920's, it was home to the biggest KKK rally ever held above the Mason Dixon line in the United States. Over 8000 people went to see a Senator from Alabama speak. Some will claim this additive still runs in the political blood of some politicians from the area.

Glocester was originally named for **Henry Stuart**, the Duke of Gloucester. In 1806, they got tired of being confused with the town in Massachusetts with the same name so they went looking through ancient English texts and realized they could take the "u" out and differentiate themselves. Glocester has always been a home to the folks who like to act out. Try to stay a loyalist while living in Newport during Colonial Times? Get sent to Glocester. Taking part in a Calvinist Civil War? Get sent to Glocester.

This spirit of acting out led to 2 important events. The 1841 **Dorr Rebellion** started in Glocester. **Thomas Wilson Dorr** was not cool with the small rural cabal running the state at the time. He wanted folks to be franchised. Then on July 4th, 1926 **The Ancient and Horribles Brigade** became an annual tradition. Other communities had been doing this kind of satire since the 1870's but they were never this organized or successful.

As you might imagine, the spirit of acting out has also affected schools in the area from time to time. Because the area is 98% white, you always have to be cautious when you hear about "breaking news." Just like the KKK rally a century ago, many are waiting for an "Incel gathering" in the modern era.

If you're looking for a truly rural area in Rhode Island furthest away from the oceans, this is the spot. That has historically attracted two kinds of people. On one hand, you get intensely hard workers who expect nothing from the government. They expect to totally rely on themselves. On the other hand, you can get some discontent types.

Pirate Hicks had a bunch of aliases. We will go with **Albert Hicks** (1820 - July 16, 1860) for now. He was one of 7 kids and the moment he got to school he started fighting. Not surprising, he went to jail the first time as a teenager. Less surprisingly, being a kid, he was sexually assaulted on a daily basis. When he got out, he promised a war against the entire human race.

The next 2 decades were exactly that on the high seas. He might have killed close to 100 people. Lord knows he paid for that many prostitutes. After 20 years, he decided to settle down with a young wife who knew nothing of his past. Things were fine until he got a gig on a Schooner. Of course he killed again. This time, thanks to a boat accident during the murder, he would be held accountable. He was tried and executed, on Friday the 13th of all days. Before his death, he cut a "wax figure" deal with P.T. Barnum.

It is not often we get to talk about direct descendants of **Roger Williams. Arthur Steere** (1865-1943) is one of them. He set an early record by owning 1000 acres of land joined together in several different towns. He is who the state bought the land off of to create the **Scituate Reservoir**. As a State Senator, lumber yards and property rights were his thing. I think a trip to **Harmony Chapel Cemetery** is in order.

We need to take care of somebody who never got proper credit. Ever hear the saying "the whole Fraternity of Noise"? Lots of folks attribute that to the 100 dollar bill guy. It was actually said by Dr. Solomon Drowne (March 11, 1753 - February 5, 1834.) After an amazing medical career and lots of charitable contributions, he decided to retire to a farm in Foster.

The next time I desire an environment where I need free thought, I know where I'm headed. The area also provides a reminder that sometimes the stuff you concentrate on all the time is not where your mind should be. The need to slow down should never be ignored.

The Mansions

In the days before GPS, the moment a person arrived in Newport who had never visited before they went looking for someone to ask "How do we get to the Mansions?" We would tell them and then always throw in the "Don't forget, they're only Summer Cottages" line. I guess now the moment a Newport vacation is planned Google Maps is consulted.

In the modern era, mansions are surrounded by fences and that's after you make the journey up the 2-mile driveway. One thing that makes the Newport Mansions special is they are right there to be seen from front in back. In the old days, which meant it was hard to keep secrets. If some-one was rowdy at a party the night before or "passed out" in the wrong house, the whole neighborhood would know. Come to think of it, parts of Newport are still like that.

The **Preservation Society of Newport County** is the nonprofit or-ganization that has the mission to preserve and protect 11 of the man-sions. Seven of them are national landmarks. If you enjoy visits to the mansions and adjoining properties, you really should stop by the Preser-vation Society and say hello. Yes, from time to time, you might have a political squabble with someone connected to the Preservation Society but always remember that their heart is in the right place.

Not only do they offer tours, but they offer lectures where you will learn all kinds of things you never would have thought to ask. Your new-found knowledge will magically spring up as you walk through life and guide you. A trip through Marble House immediately comes to mind. Katherine and George Warren inspired others to help them found the Society in 1945. It would be hard to argue that any other American municipality is more "historically intact" than the city of Newport.

Marble House reminds everybody why it's fun to have money. Think about your last birthday present. Was it a mansion? When Alva Vanderbilt turned 39, William Vanderbilt took his wife by the property and said, "See what I'm about to build for you?"

Richard Morris Hunt was the architect. Marble House is going to break the dam open. Newport was a colony and had nice wooden houses. Then Marble House happened. It was like a competition started.

From the outside, it looks like it has two levels but it actually has 4. Marble House also started the trend of having the servants live up on the 3rd floor with the kitchen down in the basement. If it feels French inspired that's because it is. You will also notice the number of times William Vanderbilt and "WV" were carved into different spots. Every year, fundraisers and the like are held in the property. In the selfie era, multiple people make sure they're next to the WV's when they take a photo.

Chateau-sur-Mer was designed by Seth C. Bradford for William Shepard Wetmore. Fall River Granite was the building material chosen. If stenciling, wallpaper, and ceramics are your thing, it is going to make you incredibly happy. You will also have moments of "What were they thinking back then?

After its original building in 1852, the home was remodeled in 1870. Part of the plan was to make the property livable year-round. It is important to remember as you walk through the other mansions to always remember "this was somebody's vacation spot." The folks at the time had an obsession with the sky. For that reason, this home features a great hall with a 45-foot ceiling. George Peabody Wetmore, the original owner's son, served as both Rhode Island Governor and United States Senator while he lived in the home.

Rosecliff features the largest ballroom in Newport but that's not what gets the attention. Remember I told you about the Rochambeau statue? Would you like to see the indoor version? Just looking at the heart shaped grand staircase can take you back in time.

Stanford White was the architect this time. Theresa Fair Olerichs, "Tessie" if you were one of her crew, had a thing for the Grand Trianon which is the garden retreat at Versailles. She actually met her husband while he was playing tennis at the Newport Casino.

Rosecliff is a major celebrity and movie attraction. Harry Houdini performed there. Multiple movies have been shot on location there including The Great Gatsby, True Lies, Amistad, and 27 Dresses. If you need to escape reality for a little while, it is a great place to visit.

The Elms is what happens when you like 18th Century architecture but want Gilded Age technology. The art inside the mansion is amazing. The grounds have a very structured feel. Every part of the mansion gives the impression of being "well thought out"

Mr. and Mrs. Edward Julius Berwind, who were coal barons, hired architect Horace Trumbauer. The French chateau d'Asnières was his inspiration. Allard and Sons of Paris were brought in as the interior designers. Mrs. Berwind already had quite the collection of paintings and ceramics. When you stop by, make sure you check out the bronze sculptures out on the terraces.

If you've heard me speak before, you know towards the end of that episode a crow flew down out of the sky and told me, "We would kill you if you were still qualified." As weird as it was to hear a crow speak English, I spent the rest of the day wondering why I wasn't qualified any longer. That incident happened in front of The Elms.

Kingscote was the first mansion to be designed with cottage intent. Southern Planter George Noble Jones was fascinated by Bellevue Avenue. He hired architect Richard Upjohn to design a cottage in the Gothic Revival Style.

The house had a makeover in 1876, which included a new dining room. The goal then was to merge traditional Colonial American designs with other styles. That's one of the reasons the opalescent glass bricks were installed by Louis Comfort Tiffany. The glass bricks combined with the Gothic Revival styling can be a major source of inspiration.

The **Issac Bell House** is an immediate draw for every student of architecture who visits the city of Newport. The Preservation Society also believes this to be the case. When they acquired it, it was barely furnished. They have kept it that way so the emphasis stays on the architecture.

Isaac Bell was in the cotton industry. He hired McKim, Mead, and White in 1883. The goal seems to have been to create a uniquely American Style. They succeeded.

Chepstow was designed by George Champlin Mason. Edmund Schermerhorn needed a summer place to play. He was a cousin of Mrs. Astor. The home was acquired by Ms. Emily Morris Gallatin in 1911. Chepstow refers to the town in Wales that the family came from.

Hunter House is more than likely the Newport property that benefitted the most from Newporter's attitudes in the 1800's towards religious freedom. The Georgian Colonial Architecture immediately stands out. Back in the 1700's, Jonathan Nichols Jr. originally built the first stage of the property. Unfortunately, he passed away just a couple of years after he was finished.

Colonel Joseph Wanton Jr. added the south wing, the central chimney, and the great hall. Putting it mildly, he had a lot of projects going on. He did all this work and then ran away when the Revolution started because his heart was where it was. While he was gone, Admiral de Ternay, Commander of the French Fleet, moved in.

When the Admiral returns home, U.S. Senator William Hunter will take control. Then the house will flip a bunch of times. In 1945, Katherine Warren is tired of history not being preserved and decides that Hunter House will make a great first effort. This is how the Preservation Society of Newport County happens. To many, forgetting how beautiful the rest of the house is, just the Cosmo Alexander and Gilbert Stuart paintings make it worth a visit.

Green Animals Topiary Garden brings up great childhood memories. One of the great things about attending both St. Philomena's and Portsmouth Abbey is that Green Animals was right around the corner. There was always a reason to point it out to my family. The best part was while the animals attracted me, the amazing display of color amongst the flowers attracted my mom.

There are only 28 official daffodil displays in the United States. This is one of them. It all started when Thomas E. Brayton, a cotton industry financier, decided that he needed a summer cottage but he wanted it to be more quiet and closer to his business interests in Fall River, Massachusetts. It was his daughter Alice who turned her gardening hobby and need to bring people together into one of the most amazing topiary displays you'll ever see.

Astor's **Beechwood** was purchased by William Backhouse Astor Jr., John Jacob Astor's grandson, 1881. His wife Caroline thought so much of this that she requested that you refer to her as "The Mrs. Astor." She was the driving force behind putting together the 400, her elite social circle, to eat and drink with her for 8 weeks every summer.

Belcourt Castle was designed by Richard Morris Hunt for Oliver Belmont. Yes, this is the family the Belmont Stakes is named after. That would explain all the carriage and horse references throughout the home. It too was supposed to be in use 6 to 8 weeks a year and then it was over. Mr. Belmont had quite the life. He was getting divorced because his wife, Sara Swan Whiting, had a child that he said wasn't his. If that weren't entertaining enough, just as construction was being completed, Mr. Belmont got mugged. He wouldn't see his new playpen until a year after it was completed.

Mr. Belmont ended up marrying Alva Vanderbilt, the former wife of William Kissam Vanderbilt, in 1896. Yes, he married the woman from down the block. I am sure nobody talked about that. She arrives and immediately begins redecorating.

The house is going to flip around a couple of times, and be uninhabited for long periods until the Tinney's from Cumberland buy it in 1956. Over time, Mrs. Tinney will make a number of changes, the biggest one being the gates. She wants the tallest gates in Newport and installs them from Portsmouth.

The home is different from most mansions for two huge reasons. Most mansions are empty or only have paid staff living stashed away upstairs. The Tinneys are showing the home while living in it. Harle Tinney often gave the tours herself.

The Breakers was built by Cornelius Vanderbilt. At various times, he was the richest man in America. You will be struck first by the Italian palazzo design. Richard Morris Hunt will once again be the architect. However in this case he will have some special instructions. This construction will be replacing a home destroyed by fire. Steel, brick, and limestone is the order of the day. There will be other fire precautions built in as well.

Out of the 70 rooms, 48 are bedrooms. Twenty-seven fireplaces are featured. It was one of the first buildings in Newport with electricity. In 1948, the Preservation Society was given permission to give tours. In 1972, the Preservation Society bought the property. While that is true, throughout the 70's and 80's, thanks to Gloria Vanderbilt, members of the original family were always in the neighborhood.

Rough Point is a Newport Restoration Foundation property. It is amazing inside, it is amazing outside, it looks amazing whether you view it from an airplane or a boat. Even the piano stool is worth taking a look at. Doris Duke was an amazing human. Well, maybe except for one moment which is why Rough Point is on the list.

On October 7, 1966 Ms. Duke and her interior designer Eduardo Tirella were headed out to dinner. They were in a station wagon. He gets out to open the gates. She slides over to drive the station wagon through the gates. Before he can get done, she smashes the car into him and crushes his body causing his death up against a tree.

There were rumors they were not getting along. However, the Police Chief declared it to be an accident. Then a bunch of coincidences followed. That is the night the Newport Restoration Foundation came into being. A couple of days later, Ms. Duke magically contributes $25,000 for Cliff Walk restoration. A few months later, the Chief resigned. Do not fret, this is just controversial. There are still some actual murder mysteries coming up.

I decided to list the **Newport Cliff Walk** in the mansions section because it is how most folks experience the mansions the first time. Back in the timeshare days when I had the info booth by the wave statue folks would stop by every day and ask "Hey Bobby, we only got a couple of hours free tomorrow, we know where the mansions are, but which mansion should we visit?" I would tell them to walk the Cliff Walk and they'd know immediately.

This is one of the huge ways Newport is different. In most non-downtown environments, you need binoculars to see a famous home unless you're taking a tour. In Newport, you can get an intimate look of almost every property. This also makes them feel much more like "neighbors" instead of attractions.

I feel sad now that I took jogging on the Cliff Walk each day in my early 40's for granted. Even on days I just needed an idea, it was a great place to walk. In the last few years, there have been a couple of collapses. I hope the fundraising goes well and problems get fixed. It is an experience everyone should enjoy multiple times.

Please keep in mind that this is the Mansions section. There are plenty of other buildings that we'll talk about. I just ask for your patience because I know some folks might be on the way to Newport, or already be there, see this in a store and hope it can help them plan the rest of the day. Just like the old days, I'd say go hit the Cliff Walk first.

Question: Can you identify this mansion in downtown Newport?
Answer on page 162

Underrated Beaches

I know some of you don't like crowds. You have no desire to hang with the cool kids. At the same time, you still want to go to the beach. You want to lay in the sand or ride the waves. You just don't want to do it with other humans around you. I can give you some hints on that one.

I didn't even know **Buttonwoods Beach** at Warwick City Park existed until I got here therefore you need to thank my wife. The park covers 126 acres and features 3 miles of bicycle paths. There are also 3 ballfields if you want to play catch.

You can never or mention **3rd Beach** in Middletown enough. Half mile of shoreline with picnic tables. Best part of all, great blues fishing in early September.

Are you a do-it-your-selfer type? **Teddy's Beach** is just the spot for you. It's located in Island Park. Even trash is carry in/carry out. If drinking is your thing, there are some wonderful establishments within walking distance.

Don't mind if the beach is rocky? Want it surrounded by private beaches? **South Shore** in Little Compton fits this description. It's also great for people watching.

Plan to stay in Rhode Island for the summer and want to see things at an angle most others don't? Make sure you have at least a 30-day rental agreement renting in Jamestown and head down to **Mackerel Cove**. From personal experience, I can tell you that the sunrise on this beach is amazing.

What is the quietest opportunity? **Camp Cronin** in Narragansett is quiet and pet friendly. Also a good fishing spot when September rolls around. Yes, it is a little rocky.

Once again, I hope this list finds that "just right" opportunity when you need things to be a little calmer.

There is a sailing pavilion at Brown University named after Ted Turner.

America's Cup

The America's Cup hasn't been in Newport since 1983. That doesn't mean America hasn't won it. That means the New York Yacht Club hasn't won it. As you might imagine, some weird stuff goes along with this race. I figure I'd mention a few of the more entertaining items. (Yes, I did celebrate with the Aussies in '83 the night they won. Most local kids who had any access to Newport did as well.)

Ever wonder where blimp names come from? Since 1928, they've come off of America's Cup Yachts. That would include Stars & Stripes.

The Aussies didn't like having the Cup as well. They have a rock band called Pond. A couple of years ago they put out a song called America's Cup. In it, they complained about the gentrification of Fremantle. Who knew?

Long before TBS happened, Ted Turner was an America's Cup owner. Last time he won was Courageous in 1977. Makes you wonder what happens if he wins in 1983 instead of the Freedom Syndicate.

It seems there are more rules for yacht racing than for the NFL. I won't even cause your eyes to glaze over by explaining what calculation you need to do to get to 12 meters. Once the Catamarans came out, this all got worse.

This all started in 1851 because a bunch of go-getters won an event on the Isle of Wight. They thought the trophy should be donated in perpetuity for a competition every few years. They had no idea what it was going to become.

It should be noted that it is the oldest international competition held in any sport. Problem is, not a lot of folks get a chance to sail. So when they're watching what's happening, they can't identify with it so easily.

Would I love to sail on a 12 Meter Yacht again? Of course, I would. Do we have to tie up the whole city so the right people are in the neighborhood so chance happenings like that can come to life? That's asking a lot. If you're wondering about Catamarans, there was a local company that offered daily tours in them during my timeshare career. While the feeling is awesome, it's not as awesome as a 12 Meter which I haven't been on in 4 decades. So it is conflicting.

Legends

Rhode Island is all about water. Water back in the 1700 and 1800's meant Pirates. Pirates lead to hidden treasure. Or people just make up stories to see if you'll chase them. Just like I did in the Spiritual Women section, I want to present the most probable instead of just throwing all of them against the wall.

Some folks want to find the Gaspee itself. Some folks are a little greedier and want to head out to Greene Island, a lot smaller than the 14 acres it started out as, and find buried treasure. Some grandparents have been caught half kidding about the whole thing.

Soldiers on both sides during the Revolutionary War buried their valuables. That's why so many "caches" of items from the era have been found in Potterville off Town Farm Road. The rumor is there's a big score yet to be had based on some diary entries that have been discovered.

Charles Harris was a pirate. He was finally caught and hanged in 1723 at the base of the Newport Cliffs. Reportedly he had a treasure chest with him. The story goes that they found one in 1949 matching the general description but before they could recover it, the sand and the tide made that impossible. That would all suggest it is still there.

Captain Kidd supposedly had so much time on his hands, all he did was bury stuff. Whether it's Watch Hill or Block Island, the Captain left something behind. I wonder if he regretted any of those choices?

What are Arabian coins doing on a farm in Middletown? Is this the result of a 300-year-old swindle attempt? Or were Arabian tourists here long before we thought?

Not too far away in Portsmouth **General Richard Prescott** had his farm. He was into gold coins. He wasn't into treasure chests so they could be spread all over the place.

If you believe the legends, maybe it's time to buy a metal detector and sweep everywhere. How many gold or Arabian coins do you have to find before one of those things pays for itself?

Question: What style of architecture is the Isaac Bell House?
Answer on page 162

Spiritual Women

Rhode Island has a reputation as a progressive place. But no matter where you go or how progressive the place, some truths never change. When it comes to women, that is true in Rhode Island. They are often left without a voice, if not outright assaulted and silenced. Because of the way the universe works, the silenced sometimes have a louder voice in the afterlife and continue to leave their mark.

Mercy Brown born in 1793. Tuberculosis ravaged her family. Many took this as a sign that the undead were upon them. **Mercy** would die from the disease at 19 and be buried in the **Chestnut Hill Baptist Cemetery.** A few months after she died, her father was convinced by friends that something supernatural was up. The bodies would be exhumed. Most of his kids decomposed as expected. **Mercy** did not. Not only was she not decomposed, there was still blood in her heart. Many thought she was a vampire. Her organs were burned and her ashes were mixed into a medicinal tonic for her youngest brother to drink to stop him from getting the disease. He died two months later anyway.

Mercy was not the only spirit hanging around. In 1908, the **Ladd School** was developed for the "feeble minded." If you were a young lady that might mean you slept around more than society thought you should. The school never had enough staff or rooms. A number of kids hung themselves by accident in the shower. Young women were raped and there was no one to report it to. It is said if you walk by the school at night, not only can you hear the young women moaning and screaming, you can hear what sounds like a shower running in the background.

Dolly Ellen Cole was so loved by her community that the people of Foster nicknamed her "The Foster Witch." That all seemed fine until a day in 1865 when someone burned her house down while she was out collecting food and water. I suppose she could have gotten over that if her daughter, a true look-alike, didn't die in the fire. **Dolly** went over to a stream by **Tucker Hollow Road** and cast a curse. She wanted everyone to remember what happened to her. Some townsfolk heard about the curse and she was ambushed and killed with pitchforks. A few months passed and her body magically appeared by what is now known as **Dolly Cole Brook.** Many folks claim to have seen her. I don't think she's going away any time soon.

You change the management of a building and that doesn't mean that the ghost goes away. There is a **La Quinta Hotel** in Warwick that used to be a **Fairfield Inn and Suites.** When it was a **Fairfield,** a young lady committed suicide in one of the rooms. She hangs out in room 316 and tries to reenact the suicide daily with some screaming. There's also an old farmer that hangs out in 506, but he's quiet and just nods a lot.

Some people are a lot more direct in who they dislike. **Mad Maggie** lives in the Block Island Southeast Lighthouse. Her husband broke her neck at the bottom of the stairs. He claimed it was a suicide but ended up with a guilty verdict anyway. She only messes with guys who are around the building at night.

One thing I can guarantee you is that every Newport Mansion has been subject to multiple séances. The most reliable ghost is over at **The Breakers. Alice Vanderbilt** lost many people she loved, including her kids. It's almost as if starting in life she built a prison for her emotions. Now they are stuck and will not move on. Did I mention she's the great grandmother of a guy who works over at CNN?

Yes, there are louder ghosts and more spectacular stories out there. The problem is they all seem to be stories. These ghosts punch the clock and put in a real workday. I respect a good work ethic.

118

Do You Know Rhode Island?

Rhode Island is home to the **"Cemetery of the Innocents"** in Newport, a colonial era cemetery that is the final resting place for thousands of African slaves and free blacks.

Providence is famous for its unique art installation called **WaterFire.** Created by artist Barnaby Evans, WaterFire features more than eighty bonfires lit on the surface of the three rivers that run through downtown Providence. The fires create a mesmerizing display of light and provide a romantic and enchanting atmosphere. The event attracts thousands of visitors and is a must-see experience.

The John O. Pastore papers are held at the Providence College Library

The collection of John O. Pastore (1907-2000) highlights a long career in public service at the state and national level, spanning from his time as Rhode Island State Representative, Rhode Island Assistant Attorney General, Governor of Rhode Island, and United States Senator. The bulk of the collection deals with the later part of his years in Washington. This material consists of documents on Committee service (e.g., Joint Committee on Atomic Energy and Senate Commerce Subcommittee on Communications), public and private speeches, significant correspondence with prominent political figures and organizational leaders,

119

legislative reports, congressional records, election materials, and photographs.

John Brown, second of the four surviving sons of James Brown II, and the most intellectually curious. In 1769 he took part in observations of the transit of Venus across the sun. Transit Street in Providence is named for the event. Brown was the architect of several of Providence's landmark buildings, including Brown University's University Hall, Market House, the First Baptist Meeting House, and John Brown House. The private residence he designed in 1774 still stands at 50 South Main Street in Providence.

Moses Brown youngest of the four surviving sons of James Brown II. He and his brothers co-founded the College in the English Colony of Rhode Island and Providence Plantations, later known as Brown University in 1764. He also founded the New England Yearly Meeting School in 1784, which later became known as the Moses Brown School.

Like his father and brothers, Moses spent the beginning of his adult life engaging in the economic and political life of the Colony, but following a disastrous 1764 slaving expedition, in which more than half of enslaved Africans perished, he began to withdraw from business in general and the slave trade in particular. In 1774 he became a Quaker and directed a great deal of his energies toward the abolition of slavery.

The Tavares brothers—Ralph, Butch, Tiny, Pooch, and Chubby—grew up in Fox Point in Providence. In the mid-seventies they scored twelve top-15 rhythm and blues hits in a row, including "Ain't No Woman Like the One I Got," "Free Ride," and "Heaven Must Be Missing an Angel (Part 1)." Prior to their fame, they were once arrested for singing on a Providence street corner.

Brad Faxon and Billy Andrade professional golfers and Rhode Island natives are co-founders, of the Andrade-Faxon Charities for Children.

Robert Duane Ballard a Ph.D. in marine geology and geophysics from the University of Rhode Island (1974), a 2004 appointment as professor of oceanography, and current tenure as Director of the Institute for

Archaeological Oceanography at URI's Graduate School of Oceanography and the discoverer of the Titanic and PT-109 .

Joseph Michael Banigan Irish-born businessman and industrialist, co-founder of the U.S. Rubber Company and its president from 1893 to 1896, and a prime benefactor of Rhode Island's Catholic churches.

Maximilian Berlitz a linguist and founder of the Berlitz Language Schools, the first of which he established in Providence in 1878. The Berlitz Method teaches language through immersion rather than focusing on grammar or strict translation.

Bill Osmanski was born in Providence Rhode Island "Bullet Bill" Osmanski, a high school All-State fullback in Rhode Island, starred for nationally ranked Holy Cross College in 1936-1938. The Crusaders won twenty-three, lost three in that span. Osmanski was named an All-American his senior year. He moved on to pro football with the Chicago Bears after George Halas convinced him that he could study dentistry at nearby Northwestern University. In his rookie season, he led the NFL in rushing with 699 yards in 121 carries. He played on four world championship teams in his seven-year career with the Bears. Osmanski died in 1996.

East Side Mansions: The East Side of Providence is home to some of the most elegant mansions and historic residences in the city. Benefit Street, often referred to as "Mile of History," showcases exquisite architecture from various periods, including Colonial, Federal, and Victorian. Many of these houses have been preserved and are now occupied by private residents, while others serve as museums or educational institutions.

Providence has a thriving culinary scene, with numerous award-winning restaurants and talented chefs. The city is particularly known for its diverse range of cuisines, including Italian, Portuguese, and Southeast Asian. Federal Hill, also known as "Little Italy," is a neighborhood filled with Italian restaurants and specialty shops, making it a haven for food enthusiasts.

One of Providence's hidden treasures is **Roger Williams Park**, spanning over four hundred acres. This expansive urban park offers a variety of attractions, including a zoo, botanical gardens, ponds, walking trails, and picnic areas. It's a perfect place for outdoor recreation, family outings, and enjoying nature within the city.

Providence was the hometown of renowned author **H.P. Lovecraft**, known for his influential works of horror fiction. Lovecraft's stories, such as "The Call of Cthulhu" and "At the Mountains of Madness," drew inspiration from his surroundings in Providence, with references to local landmarks and fictionalized versions of the city. Fans of Lovecraft can explore the Lovecraft Arts & Sciences Council and take walking tours to discover these connections.

The Preservation Society of Newport County's newest tour, **"Beneath the Breakers,"** gives guests a chance to explore the inner workings of the luxurious and cutting-edge Vanderbilt mansion. The tour, which started in early January, takes visitors under the mansion to the boiler room, the central spot that powered the five floors of the Vanderbilt's' summer home. Visitors then walk through a 360-foot tunnel that connects to the basement, a spot the Preservation Society uses to display construction techniques and systems along with their modern counterparts.

There is an amazing museum located on the **Johnson & Wales University** campus. Filled with everything from antique kitchen tools and a real 1950s-era diner to an incredible display of decorated cakes made by the students at the university, this museum gives an in-depth look into the evolution of the modern-day culinary landscape. Many popular chefs have graduated from Johnson & Wales and their achievements are celebrated in the revolving displays, Richard J.S. Gutman, director and curator of the museum, is the world's foremost expert on diners. Erin Williams, the collections manager, can explain the stories behind the displays in the museum's collection, like this Thomas Jefferson dinner invitation with a delivery schedule written in Jefferson's own hand. Little surprises like this are everywhere in the culinary museum.

Established in 1877, the **Rhode Island School of Design Museum** is the foremost art museum in southeastern New England. Together with the Rhode Island School of Design, this fascinating museum houses

100,000 objects—ranging from contemporary works to ancient Egyptian artifacts and the largest historic Japanese wooden sculpture in the United States. The museum is also a trove of works of many major figures of art history like **Cezanne, Monet, Matisse, Pollock, Picasso, Warhol, and van Gogh,** to name a few. Named one of the Best University Art Museums in America by Architectural Digest, the RISD Museum is housed in a beautifully designed building that complements its dazzling array of collections.

The Providence Library Company was founded in 1753 by a group of Providentians who wanted to read but could not afford to have books shipped from Europe on their own. Before the city had a public lending library, this organization gave members access to the world through shared books for a small fee. The company eventually set up shop in the Athenaeum (named for Athena, Greek goddess of wisdom) in 1836. It's been an institution ever since.

Don't be daunted by the neoclassical columns and name. **The Athenaeum**, or "the Ath" as some of its regulars know it, is for everyone. On any given day, anyone can quickly visit and browse the stacks, which include gems like the 1855 edition of *Leaves of Grass* (containing notes in Walt Whitman's own handwriting), an 1830s book on astronomy, and a Regency-era book of boys' entertainments.

Artworks dominate the walls of the building. A full-length portrait of George Washington looks over the reading room, while another wall is graced with a bookplate from The Raven painted by Édouard Manet. The library has its fair share of literary history, even aside from its tomes. Poet Sarah Helen Whitman broke off her courtship with Edgar Allan Poe in the Athenaeum, and H. P. Lovecraft visited many a time and even wrote to friends about the charming little library in Providence.

The Athenaeum still functions as a library but it's also much more than that. There are musical events, parties, old-fashioned salons and speaking events, all hosted in the beautiful Victorian library stacks. The busts of Cicero and Athena even wear costumes. It serves as an important cultural space in Providence, and its public programs have earned the institution a reputation as "a 19th-century library with the soul of a 21st-century rave party."

The John Hay Library, at Brown University, has some particularly rare specimens. This library, in Providence, houses an extraordinary collection of one-of-a-kind books and manuscripts. For example, John Hay has three anthropodermic books. If you can decode the word's Greek roots, you know it means books "bound in human skin." Historically, an anatomy textbook could be bound with the skin of a cadaver, and, in a few cases, eccentrics requested that upon their deaths their skin be used to bind favorite books.

There are three books in the John Hay Library bound with human skin. Appropriately, one is the famous anatomy textbook *De Humani Corporis Fabrica* (On the Structure of the Human Body) by Andreas Vesalius. They also have two copies of Dance of Death by Hans Holbein the Younger, which were both rebound anthropodermically in 1898.

The library has other, less hair-raising collections, including the papers and personal library of John Hay, Class of 1858, who was the private secretary of Abraham Lincoln and late Secretary of State, as well as more modern treasures, such as the personal manuscripts and letters of science fiction and horror master H. P. Lovecraft.

The John Hay Library is **open to all members of the Brown community and to the general public.**

Standing twelve feet tall and standing in front of Providence's Federal Courthouse is an unusual monument constructed of steel, concrete, and used handguns. Dubbed the **"Gun Totem"** by its artist, Boris Bally, the imposing obelisk was constructed in 2001 with guns from a firearm buy-back program in Pittsburgh. Altogether, more than 1,000 guns went into the construction of the pillar, which was commissioned by the Providence Parks Department. All of the guns included in the project were disabled and fossilized beneath concrete, and bits of the pillar were chipped away so people could see the deadly layer beneath its exterior.

Yawgoo Valley is Rhode Island's **only ski resort** still in operation. It is located in Exeter, south of Providence, and opened in the 1965–66 season as "Rhode Island's first chairlift served ski area." Yawgoo relies heavily on artificial snowmaking, being one of the southernmost ski areas in New England. The Ski Area operates early December through late March and the Snow Tubing Park is open late December through March. You can ski and snowboard on twelve trails spread over thirty-six acres of terrain with two double chair lifts. The snow tubing park offers two rope tows, no walking uphill! Enjoy free parking, concessions at Shredders Snack shack, and relax in the Max Lounge.

The fascinating history of textile mills in this city is so important to its inhabitants that the Rhode Island Historical Society created a museum dedicated to it. You can learn all about historical Woonsocket factory life Tuesday through Sunday at 42 South Main Street in Woonsocket. **The Museum of Work and Culture** presents the compelling story of immigrants who came to find a better life in the mill towns along the Blackstone River. Visitors recreate this journey, beginning in the Quebecois farmhouse before making their way to the workday of Woonsocket at the turn of the century. Guests explore the lives of immigrants at home, work, and school through nine immersive exhibits.

The South County Museum honors Rhode Island's rural, village and maritime history. The museum, at 115 Strathmore St., Narragansett, is located on eight acres with seven exhibit buildings, including a print shop, blacksmith forge, carpentry shop and schoolhouse. A living history farm and flower gardens are available to explore on what was once the19th-century estate of Rhode Island's Civil War-era governor William Sprague. Walking trails through woods, meadows and salt marshes are accessible from the museum. Daily admission is $12 for adults, $10 for seniors and AAA members and $5 for children 6-12. Members and children under six are free. South County Museum, a Blue Star museum, offers free admission to active-duty military personnel and their families. Exhibits are open 10 a.m. to 4 p.m. on Fridays and Saturdays during May, June, and September from 10 a.m. to 4 p.m. Tuesday through Saturday during July and August. Special arrangements can be made for October by calling the museum.

The mission of the **Tomaquag Museum**, in Exeter, is to educate the public and promote thoughtful dialogue regarding Indigenous history, culture, arts, and Mother Earth and connect to Native issues of today. Tomaquag Museum envisions its future as an Indigenous Cultural Education destination that engages visitors in thoughtful dialogue that promotes understanding and strives to create experiences that transform people's lives by broadening their perspectives, attitudes, and knowledge of Indigenous Cultures and the interrelationship with the wider world.

The Museum of Primitive Art and Culture is dedicated to commemorating the past while enriching the lives of people today. The past is not only our heritage, but also a bridge to a brighter future. Bring the past to life at the MPAC!

The **St. Ann Arts and Cultural Center** is a non-religiously affiliated, non-profit corporation dedicated to the preservation and restoration of the former St. Ann's Roman Catholic Church building located at 84 Cumberland Street, in Woonsocket, RI. It contains the largest collect of art fresco painting in America.

Question: Can you identify this monument?
Answer on page 162

Hurricane 1938

The Great New England Hurricane of 1938 wove a path of death and destruction through the city, with a tidal-wave like storm surge and wind gusts of more than 100 miles per hour. The storm's effect on Rhode Island was so severe that earthquake instruments 3,000 miles away recorded it on seismographs. Narragansett Bay took the worst hit; a storm surge of 12 to 15 feet destroyed most coastal homes, marinas and yacht clubs. Downtown Providence, Rhode Island was submerged under a storm tide of nearly 20 feet. This boat landed in downtown Providence.

Providence Library Digital Collection

Do You Know?

Rhode Island got the worst of it. It is believed 229 Rhode Islanders died during the Hurricane of 1938. Parts of downtown Providence were under 14 feet of water, with people sheltering on the second and third floors of buildings. According to the National Weather Service, a storm surge of 12 to 15 feet destroyed most coastal homes, yacht clubs and marinas on Narragansett Bay.

The photo below shows the view of a flooded parking lot near the Gaspee Street underpass, with cars under water up to their roofs. Two people are sitting on the roof of a shipping truck. A train is on the bridge above the parking lot, with people standing alongside the rails. The State House is visible in the background.

Providence Library Digital Collection

One story of thousands reported by the New England Historical Society:

Perhaps the most astounding story of the storm comes from the Moore family of Westerly, R.I. As the storm grew stronger, the family tried to evacuate their beachfront home, but could not. As the ocean waves began surging into the house, Catherine Moore recalls her father bracing against the front door literally trying to hold back the ocean.

The family moved first to the second floor and finally to the third floor to stay above the storm surge, watching as house after house succumbed and neighbors were washed away. Finally, the waves overwhelmed their own house, lifting it off its foundation.

"Next thing I knew, we were floating," Moore recalled. "We were on the water with the waves crashing over us, and part of the house still attached, one of the walls still attached to this piece of floor, and it almost acted as a sail."

In all, 10 people clung to that bit of floor as it hurtled across the Sound to land in Connecticut. There the family stepped back on to land and back into their lives.

Image from Cranston: Cars partially submerged underwater in the cove.

100 Questions and Answers

1. Which of the following states does NOT border Rhode Island?

   a) New York
   b) Pennsylvania
   c) Massachusetts
   d) Connecticut

   Answer: b) Pennsylvania (RI is surrounded by Massachusetts, New York and Connecticut.)

2. Providence has the world's largest _____ on top on the roof of one of its buildings.

   a) Bug
   b) Ice Cream Cone
   c) Hamburger
   d) Donut

   Answer: a) Bug (It's a 58" long blue termite on top of the roof of New England Pest Control in Providence.)

3. Rhode Island was the second state in the original 13 colonies.

   a) True
   b) False

   Answer: b) False (Rhode Island was the last of the original thirteen colonies to become a state.)

4. Which Rhode Island city hosted the first polo match in the US?

   a) Providence
   b) Newport
   c) Pawtucket
   d) Middletown

   Answer: b) Newport

5. The Flying Horse Carousel, the oldest continuously operating carousel in America, is in which Rhode Island village?

a) Providence
b) Cranston
c) Watch Hill
d) Warwick

Answer: c) Watch Hill (It provided its first ride way back in 1876.)

6. Which city is the International Tennis Hall of Fame located in?

a) Newport
b) Providence
c) Middletown
d) Cranston

Answer: a) Newport (The complex, the former Newport Casino, includes a museum, grass tennis courts, an indoor tennis facility, a tennis court facility, and a theatre.)

7. Which town is the oldest synagogue in the US located in?

a) Providence
b) Newport
c) Middletown
d) Narragansett

Answer: b) Newport (Tuoro Synagogue, in Newport. was founded by Roger Williams when he was expelled from Massachusetts because of his religious beliefs.)

8. The first established Baptist Church in the US is in this town?

a) Providence
b) Narragansett
c) Bourne
d) Newport

Answer: a) Providence (Rogers Williams advocated for religious freedom and established the country's first Baptist Church in 1638.)

9. Which is the state bird for Rhode Island?

a) The Red Cardinal
b) The Red Tail Hawk
c) The Red Chicken
d) The Blue Jay

Answer: c) The Red Chicken (Rhode Island Red was developed as a dual-purpose breed, to provide both meat and eggs.)

10. What is the name of the oldest operating restaurant in the US?

a) The White Horse Tavern
b) Hemenway's Restaurant
c) The Capital Grille
d) Providence Oyster Bar

Answer: a) The White Horse Tavern (Located at 26 Marlborough St, Newport) opened in 1673 is also the world's 10th oldest restaurant.

11. One of the nation's first mills sits on the Blackstone River since the 1760's and is called?

a) Greystone Mill, Greystone Ave, North Providence
b) Old Slater Mill, 67 Roosevelt Ave, Pawtucket
c) Kenyon's Grist Mill, 21 Glen Rock Rd, West Kingston
d) Lippitt Mill, 825 Main St, West Warwick

Answer: b) Old Slater Mill (It is the first water-powered cotton spinning mill in North America.)

12. The fourth-largest self-supported marble dome in the world is in which Rhode Island town?

a) Kington
b) Newport
c) Providence
d) Warwick

Answer: c) Providence (The gold coated dome supports a statue of "The Independent Man" on top on the capital building.)

13. Jackie and John F. Kennedy got married in St Mary's Roman Catholic Church in which town in Rhode Island?

a) Newport
b) Providence
c) Kington
d) Narragansett

Answer: a) Newport (Officially the Church of the Holy Name of Mary, Our Lady of the Isle, is a historic Catholic parish church complex at 14 William Street, at the corner of Spring Street and Memorial Boulevard, in Newport within the Diocese of Providence. It is the oldest Catholic parish in the state.)

14. This military fort is the largest fort on the US east coast?

a) Fort Adams
b) Fort Kearny
c) Fort Mansfield
d) Fort Church

Answer: a) Adams (The former US Army post in Newport was established on July 4, 1799, as a First System coastal fortification. It was named for President John Adams.)

15. 18.9 percent of Rhode Islanders have Italian heritage, making it the most Italian state.

a) True
b) False

Answer: a) True (Most are concentrated in the north of the state in Johnston, Cranston, and Providence.)

16. Why would you see Mr. Potato Head on a RI license plate?

a) Most potatoes are grown in Rhode Island
b) The headquarters for Hasbro Toys is in Providence
c) Mr. Potato Head was invited in Rhode Island
d) He's the state mascot

Answer: b) The headquarters for Hasbro Toys is in Providence (The toy giant has made Providence its home since 1923.)

17. In 1872, a Rhode Islander by the name of Walter Scott invented a horse drawn restaurant sparking this popular American tradition.

a) Italian Ice
b) The Pizzeria
c) The Diner
d) The Hamburger Stand

Answer: c) The Diner (1872 saw the opening of the "night lunch wagon" for those who worked and played after the restaurants had shut at 11:00pm. Its mix of open-all-hours eating and cheap, homemade food proved a hit, and the formula has been repeated ever since. Haven Bros. continues the tradition with a food truck in Providence near City Hall.)

18. The basketball technique called "the fast break" was invented in RI.

a) True
b) False

Answer: a) True (Known as the architect of modern run-and-shoot basketball, Frank Keaney's up-tempo style made use of a fast-breaking offense and a full-court defense.)

19. What is the Cliff Walk?

a) A restaurant
b) A hotel
c) A walk on the Newport coast
d) A walk on the Appalachian Trail in Rhode Island

Answer c) A walk on the Newport coast (This 4 ½ mile walk takes you along the beautiful coast and allows visitors to tour the mansions of the Vanderbilts, the Asters, the Dukes and more.)

20. Which celebrity is NOT from Rhode Island?

a) Meredith Vieira
b) Viola Davis
c) Debra Messing
d) Kathy Bates

Answer: d) Kathy Bates (All of the others are Rhode Islanders)

21. Which movie was NOT filmed in Rhode Island?

a) Me, Myself and Irene (2000)
b) Amistad (1997)
c) Good Will Hunting (1994)
d) Thirteen Days (2000)
e) True Lies (1994)

Answer: c) Good Will Hunting (This movie was filmed in Boston)

22. Which of the follow is NOT a fine dining venue in Providence?

a) Gracie's
b) Mills Tavern
c) Capriccio
d) Ken's Steak House
e) Camille's
f) Bacaro

Answer: d) Ken's Steakhouse (This restaurant is in Framingham, MA.)

23. Which of the following is NOT a top choice for pizza in Providence?

a) Flatbread Pizza Company
b) Fellini Pizzeria
c) Piemonte Pizza
d) Imbriglio's Pizzeria Napoletana Resto Bar

Answer: d) Imbriglio's Pizzeria Napoletana Resto Bar (This great pizzeria is in Newport.)

24. Where is The Exploration Center and Aquarium located?

a) Providence
b) Newport
c) Warwick
d) Middletown

Answer: b) Newport (The interactive marine science center is home to more than 40 species from Narragansett Bay and Rhode Island waters and is located at 175 Memorial Blvd., Newport.)

25. Which of the following is a zoo in Rhode Island?

a) Norman Bird Sanctuary
b) Roger Williams Park Zoo
c) Zoolab
d) A and B

Answer: d) A and B (Norman Bird Sanctuary at 583 Third Beach Road, Middletown, and Roger Williams Park Zoo at 1000 Elmwood Avenue, Providence, are a must visit!)

26. What percentage of "The Ocean State" is covered in forests?

a) 23%
b) 37%
c) 59%
d) 68%

Answer: c) 59% (Keeping it green! RI is covered in beautiful forests.)

27. The first NFL game played at night was played in Rhode Island.

a) True
b) False

Answer: a) True (In 1929 the Chicago Cardinals played the Providence Steam Roller in Providence.)

28. Which of the following is a bike path in Rhode Island?

a) Ten Mile River Greenway
b) East Bay Bike Path
c) Calf Pasture Bike Path
d) Blackstone Greenway
e) All of the above

Answer: e) All of the above (Rhode Island's beautiful landscape is the perfect setting for more than 60 miles of off-road cycling across the entire state.)

29. Which of the following is NOT a public golf course in Providence?

a) Triggs Memorial Golf Course
b) Button Hole
c) Louisquisset Golf Club
d) Wannamoisett Country Club

Answer: d) Wannamoisett Country Club (The Wannamoisett Country Club is a private golf course located in Rumford, Rhode Island, and played host to the 1931 PGA Championship.)

30. Which of the following is a public golf course in or near Warwick?

a) West Warwick Country Club
b) Midville Golf Club
c) Valley Country Club
d) Harbor Lights Dining Events Golf Marina
e) All of the above

Answer: e) All of the above (Warwick not only has an array of public golf course but also has one on the marina.)

31. Which of the following is NOT a public golf course in Rhode Island?

a) Newport Country Club
b) Jamestown Golf Course
c) Newport National Golf Club
d) Green Valley Country Club

Answer: a) Newport Country Club *(NCC is an 18-hole championship private golf course.)*

32. Which of the following is NOT a private golf course?

a) The Aquidneck Club
b) Clambake Club of Newport
c) Kings Crossing Golf Club
d) Shelter Harbor Golf Club
e) Wanumetonomy Golf and Country Club

Answer: c) Kings Crossing Golf Club (LCGC is a public 9-hole golf course which opened in 1964.)

33. Which of the following is a public tennis court in Rhode Island?

a) Centre Court Tennis Club, 55 Hospital Rd, Riverside
b) Vernon Park tennis courts, 31 Freeborn St, Newport
c) Todd Morsilli Clay Court Tennis Center, 100 Hawthorne Ave, Providence
d) Tennis Rhode Island, East Providence, 70 Boyd Ave, East Providence
e) All of the above

Answer: e) All of the above (All are beautiful courts throughout the ocean state.)

34. Which of the following is a "traditional" museum in Newport?

a) Naval War College Museum, Luce Ave, Newport
b) The Breakers, 44 Ochre Point Ave, Newport
c) Rough Point, 680 Bellevue Ave, Newport
d) Marble House, 596 Bellevue Ave, Newport
e) Belcourt of Newport, 657 Bellevue Ave, Newport

Answer: a) Naval War College Museum (The NWCM is one of 10 official American museums operated by the United States Navy. The remaining landmarks are "historical place museums" that were glorious mansions open to the public.)

35. The Newport Car Museum is the only automobile museum in Newport.

a) True
b) False

Answer: b) False (The Newport Car Museum is a celebration of the art of the car with over 72 cars on display in 114,000 square feet at all times in Portsmouth but there is also Audrain Auto Museum at the Audrain Building, 222 Bellevue Ave, Newport. It is comprised of over 160 of the rarest and most remarkable automobiles in history.)

36. Which is NOT a museum in Providence, RI?

a) RISD Museum
b) Museum of Natural History and Planetarium
c) Haffenreffer Museum of Anthropology
d) Lippitt House Museum
e) Electromagnetic Pinball Museum and Restoration

Answer: e) Electromagnetic Pinball Museum and Restoration (The museum is in in the Commerce Center in Pawtucket.)

37. What is the name of the 325-acre bird sanctuary, nature preserve, environmental education center, and museum in Middletown, RI?

a) Jackie's Bird House
b) Norman's Bird Sanctuary
c) Prescott Farm
d) Middletown Historical Society

Answer: b) Norman's Bird Sanctuary (At 583 Third Beach Road in Middletown overlooking the Atlantic Ocean, it is a wildlife sanctuary and environmental education center with more than 325 acres of diverse habitats and 7 miles of hiking trails.)

38. Which of the following is a mall for epic shopping in Rhode Island?

    a) Warwick Mall, 400 Bald Hill Rd, Warwick
    b) Providence Place, One Providence Pl, Providence
    c) The Arcade Providence, 65 Weybosset St, Providence
    d) Bellevue Gardens Shopping Center, Newport, RI
    e) Smithfield Commons, 400 Putnam Pike, Smithfield
    f) All of the above

Answer: f) All of the above (All the shopping centers listed are great location for epic shopping.)

39. Which of the following is NOT a gun range in Providence, RI?

    a) Providence Revolver Gun Club
    b) Massasoit Gun Club
    c) Elite Indoor Gun Range
    d) American Firearms School

Answer: d) American Firearms School (This gun range is in Massachusetts)

40. Which of the following is NOT a fishing charter in Rhode Island?

    a) Snappa Charters
    b) Tall Tailz Charters
    c) Big Game Sportfishing
    d) Kingfisher Fishing Charter

Answer: d) Kingfisher Fishing Charter (With 400 miles of coastline Rhode Island offer an array of fishing charters, but KFC operates out of Connecticut.)

41. What town has the oldest house of worship?

a) Warwick
b) Providence
c) Newport
d) Narragansett

Answer: c) Newport (The Quaker Meeting House, 1699.)

42. What RI town has the current oldest schoolhouse in the US?

a) Portsmouth
b) Cranston
c) Pawtucket
d) Providence

Answer: a) Portsmouth (The schoolhouse opened in 1716.)

43. The first townhouse was built in which Rhode Island city?

a) Providence
b) Newport
c) Middletown
d) Charleston

Answer: b) Newport (In 1750, the first townhouse was built at 57 Farewell Street, Newport.)

44. The first gas-illuminated streetlights in the US were lit where?

a) Charlestown
b) Providence
c) Newport
d) Kingston

Answer: c) Newport (The streetlights were lit in 1803 on Pelham Street.)

45. Which of the following is the largest city population wise?

a) Providence
b) Warwick
c) Newport
d) Cranston

Answer: a) Providence (Providence is the largest populated city in Rhode Island with 188,812 residents.) (2020)

46. Which of the following is the second largest city in Rhode Island?

a) Warwick
b) Providence
c) Newport
d) Middleton

Answer: a) Warwick (It is the second largest city in the state, with 83,000 people.) (2010)

47. Which of the following Rhode Island airports is an International Airport and can accommodate commercial aircraft?

a) Block Island Airport
b) Newport Airport
c) Rhode Island T.F. Green
d) Westerly Airport

Answer: c) Rhode Island T.F. Green (6 miles south of the state's capital, Providence, T.F. Green International opened in 1931. The airport was named for former Rhode Island governor and longtime Senator Theodore Francis Green.)

48. What is the total number of railroads operating in Rhode Island?

a) Three
b) Five
c) Seven
d) Ten

Answer: b) Five (RI has two freight railroad operations and three passage railroad operates, including Amtrak and commuter.)

49. Which of the following is NOT a top hotel in Providence?

a) Omni Providence Hotel
b) Graduate Providence
c) The Dean Hotel
d) WoodSpring Suites Providence

Answer: d) WoodSpring Suites Providence (W.S.P is more motel level accommodations while the remaining are top level hotels)

50. Which is NOT a mansion of the wealthy turned into a hotel?

a) Hotel Viking, 1 Bellevue Ave.
b) The Vanderbilt, Auberge Resorts Collection, 41 Mary St.
c) The Chanler at Cliff Walk, 117 Memorial Boulevard
d) The Brenton Hotel, 31 America's Cup Ave.

Answer: e) The Brenton Hotel (The Brenton Hotel is excellent but is not a former mansion.)

51. Which of the following is NOT a top hotel in Middletown?

a) The Sea Breeze Inn, 147 Aquidneck Ave.
b) Mystic Marriott Hotel & Spa, 625 North Road
c) Newport Beach Hotel and Suites, 1 Wave Ave.
d) The Carriage House Inn, 93 Miantonomi Ave.

Answer: b) Mystic Marriott Hotel & Spa (Though it is an excellent hotel, it is in Connecticut.)

52. Which of the following is a hotel in Warwick?

a) NYLO Providence Warwick Hotel
b) Hyatt Place
c) Radisson Hotel
d) Hilton Garden Inn
e) All of the above

Answer: d) All of above (All of the listed hotels are in Warwick.)

53. Which of the following is a library in Newport?

a) Naval Hospital Medical Library, 43 Smith Rd.
b) Redwood Library and Athenaeum, 50 Bellevue Ave.
c) McKillop Library, 100 Ochre Point Ave.
d) Newport Public Library, 300 Spring St.
e) All of the above

Answer: e) All of the above (Though Newport is not the largest city it has its share of libraries)

54. Which library is NOT a public library located in Providence?

a) Rhode Island State Library, 82 Smith St, Providence
b) Providence Public Library, 150 Empire St, Providence
c) John Carter Brown Library, 94 George St, Providence
d) Johnson & Wales University Library, 111 Dorrance St #2807, Providence

Answer: d) Johnson & Wales University Library (This a private library for students at the university only.)

55. Which of the following is NOT a steakhouse in Providence?

a) Fleming's Prime Steakhouse & Wine Bar
b) Iron Works
c) The Capital Grille
d) Ten Prime Steak & Sushi

Answer: b) Iron Works (Iron Works is great steakhouse but it's located in Warwick, RI.)

56. Which of the following is NOT a steakhouse in Warwick?

a) Texas Roadhouse
b) LongHorn Steakhouse
c) Shogun
d) The Greenwood Inn

Answer: a) Texas Roadhouse (TX Roadhouse is in East Greenwich.)

57. Which of the following is NOT a steakhouse in Newport?

a) Brick Alley Pub & Restaurant, 140 Thames St.
b) Clarke Cooke House, 24 Bannister's Wharf
c) The Mooring Seafood Kitchen & Bar, 1 Sayers Wharf
d) Midtown Oyster Bar, 345 Thames St.
e) Malt, 150 Broadway

Answer: c) The Mooring Seafood Kitchen & Bar (Great place in Newport, RI, but the cuisine and menu is full American with seafood.)

58. Which of the following is NOT an Italian restaurant in Cranston?

a) Antonio's Trattoria, 1710 Cranston St, Cranston
b) L'Osteria Ristorante, 1703 Cranston St #5013, Cranston
c) Iannuccilli Restaurant, 1791 Cranston St, Cranston
d) Marchetti's Restaurant, 1463 Park Ave, Cranston
e) None of the above

Answer: e) None of the above (Rhode Island is known for its Italian restaurant and listed above are some of the best in Cranston.)

59. Which of the following is NOT an Italian restaurant in Providence?

a) Joe Marzilli's Old Canteen Italian Restaurant, 120 Atwells Ave.
b) Capriccio, 2 Pine St.
c) Pane e Vino, 365 Atwells Ave.
d) Cassarino's Restaurant, 177 Atwells Ave.
e) Il Fornello Italian Restaurant, 16 Josephine St.
f) Massimo Ristorante, 134 Atwells Ave.

Answer: e) Il Fornello Italian Restaurant (This is a great restaurant, but it's located in North Providence. OK... I am splitting hairs.)

60. Which of the following is not a public beach in Narragansett?

a) Scarborough State Beach
b) Lucy Vincent Beach
c) Kelly Beach
d) Salty Brine State Beach
e) Roger Wheeler State Beach

Answer: b) Lucy Vincent (Great beach on Martha's Vineyard.)

61. Which of the following is not a public beach in Charlestown?

a) East Beach
b) Ninigret Beach
c) Kelly Beach
d) Blue Shutters Beach
e) West Beach

Answer: c) Kelly Beach (This wonderful beach is in Narragansett.)

62. Which of the following is not a public beach in Newport?

a) Gooseberry Beach
b) King Park Beach
c) Bailey Beach
d) Second Beach

Answer: d) Second Beach (Great beach in Middletown!)

63. Which of the following is NOT a live theater venue in Providence?

a) Columbus Theatre
b) Firehouse Theater
c) The Wilbury Theatre Group
d) Trinity Repertory Company
e) Providence Performing Arts Center

Answer: b) Firehouse Theatre (Providence is known for its theatre district, but this theatre is in Newport)

64. Which of the following is NOT a live music venue in Providence?

a) Fete Music Hall
b) BLACK
c) The Strand Ballroom
d) Dusk
e) The Parlour Providence

Answer: b) BLACK (The music venue offers dine-in and take-out in the great town of Woonsocket.)

65. You can solve a murder mystery while you dine in Newport.

a) True
b) False

Answer: a) True (Newport Murder Mystery Company located at 2 Sunnyside Pl, Newport, is a dinner theatre.)

66. Which of the following is NOT a rock-climbing venue in RI?

a) Hanging Rock, Middleton
b) Central Rock Gym, 275 W Natick Rd, Warwick
c) Rock Spot Climbing, Providence and Lincoln
d) Rock Spot Climbing, 1174 Kingstown Rd, Peace Dale

Answer: a) Hanging Rock (Hanging Rock is a walking trail, while the remaining choices are indoor facilities.)

67. All the following are bowling venues in Cranston except?

a) Bowlero Cranston, 1450 Elmwood Ave
b) Lang's Bowlarama, 225 Niantic Ave
c) Legion Bowl and Billiards, 661 Park Ave
d) Dudek's Bowling Lanes, 409 Child St

Answer: d) Dudek's Bowling Lanes (This alley is in Warren)

68. How many professional sports teams does Rhode Island have?

a) One
b) Three
c) Six
d) Eight

Answer: a) One (Rhode Island has a semi-professional hockey team named the Providence Bruins.)

69. How many four-year universities are there in Rhode Island?

a) 10
b) 13
c) 25
d) 33

Answer: b) 13 (There are 13 four-year colleges in Rhode Island, and a total of 25 colleges and universities. Rhode Island has 3 public and 22 private higher education institutions.)

70. Rhode Island is the second smallest state in the United States.

a) True
b) False

Answer: b) False (Rhode Island is the smallest state in the Union.)

71. The headquarters of CVS Health and Pharmacy Services is located in which Rhode Island town?

a) Providence
b) Newport
c) Woonsocket
d) Cranston

Answer: c) Woonsocket (The large corporate headquarters have been located in Woonsocket but CVS started in Lowell, MA.)

72. All of the following are the most dangerous animals in RI except?

a) Cougar
b) Black Bear
c) Asian giant hornet
d) Timber Rattlesnake
e) The mosquito

Answer: a) Cougar (Cougars were officially ruled extinct in 2011, but sightings are still reported.)

73. Are there wolves in Rhode Island?

a) Yes
b) No

Answer: b) No (No, wolves are no longer found in Rhode Island after being extirpated in the 19th century, though wolf-coyote hybrids (coywolves) can still be found in the wild.)

74. Are there dolphins in Rhode Island?

 a) Yes
 b) No

Answer: a) Yes (Common dolphins are the most likely dolphin species to be spotted in Narragansett Bay, usually in late fall or winter and occasionally up as far as the Providence River.)

75. Are there poisonous snakes in Rhode Island?

 a) Yes
 b) No

Answer: a) Yes (All snakes have a small amount of venom. The copperhead and the timber rattlesnake have bitten people in RI.)

76. Which of the following is NOT a whale watching tour?

 a) Seven B's V, 30 State St
 b) Snappa Charter, 33 State Street
 c) Frances Fleet, 33 State Street
 d) Whale-Watching Cruise for One, Two, or Four, 415 Main Street

Answer: d) Whale-Watching Cruise for One, Two, or Four (This charter operates out of Gloucester, MA. In Narragansett, RI, the most common species to see in the area is the finback whale, drawn to the warmer waters in the summer months. You might also see varieties like humpback whales, false killer whales, pilot whales, and more.)

77. There are three drive-in movie theatres in Rhode Island.

 a) True
 b) False

Answer: b) False (Rustic Tri-View Drive-in Theatre in Smithfield and Misquamicut Drive-In Theater in Westerly are the only two remaining drive-ins in the state.)

78. Many horse farms in Rhode Island offer riding services, but which of the following does NOT offer trail horse riding services?

a) C and L Stables, 1095 Ives Rd, East Greenwich
b) Morning Star Horse Farm, 2415 Tower Hill Road, Saunderstown
c) Sunset Stables, 1 Twin River Rd, Lincoln
d) Rustic Rides Farm, 1173 West Side Rd, New Shoreham

Answer: b) Morning Star Horse Farm (This facility offers boarding, lessons and riding but not on trails or the beach.)

79. Which is NOT an archery lane/venue where the public can practice in Rhode Island?

a) Tangy's Indoor Archery Lanes
b) Narragansett Bow Hunters Club
c) Xspot Archery
d) Archery Games Providence

Answer: c) Xspot (This archery range is in Attleboro, MA)

80. Which of the following is a cannabis dispensary open to the public in Rhode Island?

a) Thomas C. Slater Compassion Center, 1 Corliss St, Providence
b) Mother Earth Wellness Dispensary, 125 Esten Ave, Pawtucket
c) Aura of Rhode Island, Inc., 1136 Lonsdale Ave, Central Falls
d) Sweetspot Medical and Recreational Dispensary, 560 S County Trail, Exeter
e) All of the above

Answer: d) All of the above (Cannabis is legal for recreational and medical consumption and there shops across the state.)

81. How many Division 1 college baseball teams are in RI?

a) 3
b) 8
c) 10
d) 13

Answer: a) 3 (Brown University, Providence University, and Bryant University)

82. Newport Winter Festival occurs during which month?

a) December
b) January
c) February

Answer: c) February (Usually the 3rd weekend in February the festival offers a unique winter experience combining food, festivities, music, and fun for all ages.)

83. What month does the RI Brew Fest take place in Providence?

a) June
b) September
c) January
d) May

Answer: c) January (Usually held on the last Saturday in January, The RI Brew Fest is held at The WaterFire Arts Center.)

84. What month does the Annual WINEterfest takes place?

a) November
b) December
c) January
d) February

Answer: d) February (Held at Newport Vineyards in Middletown, the festival is two days full of grape stomping, wine and beer tasting and eating tasty festive treats! Enjoy live music while sipping on our local wines or fresh Taproot beer, and noshing on food created by scratch from our culinary team.)

85. The Newport Folk Festival is held the last weekend of which month?

a) October
b) March
c) May
d) July

Answer: d) July (The festival is held at Fort Adams State Park, 80 Fort Adams Rd., Newport, RI. The Newport Folk Festival was founded by George Wein in 1959.)

86. When is the Newport Jazz Festival held?

a) It changes annually.
b) It no longer happens
c) The last weekend of July or the first weekend in August
d) July 4th

Answer: c) The last weekend of July or the first weekend in August (The venue of the festival consists of three stages at three separate locations at Fort Adams.)

87. Which is NOT a top Chinese restaurant in Rhode Island?

a) P.F. Chang's, 111 Providence Pl, Providence
b) Great Taste Chinese Restaurant, 597 W Main St, New Britain
c) House of Wu, 52 Providence St, West Warwick
d) Lee's Chinese Restaurant, **376** Bullocks Point Ave, Riverside

Answer: b) Great Taste Chinese Restaurant (This restaurant is in Connecticut)

88. Which of the following is a top Indian restaurant in Rhode Island?

a) India Restaurant, 1060 Hope St, Providence
b) The Punjab Indian and Himalayan Cuisine, 1565 Plainfield Pike, Johnston
c) Rasa Restaurant, 149 Main St, East Greenwich
d) Bollywood Grill, 1764 Mendon Rd #4385, Cumberland
e) All of the above

Answer: d) All of the above (Rhode Island has great Indian food across the state.)

89. Which of the following Irish Pub restaurants is NOT located in Rhode Island?

a) O'Rourkes Bar & Grill
b) McShawn's Pub
c) The Black Rose
d) Buskers Pub and Restaurant
e) Arigna Irish Pub & Coal Fire Kitchen

Answer: c) The Black Rose *(This terrific pub is in Boston.)*

90. Which of the following Greek restaurants is NOT located in Rhode Island?

a) Andrea's Providence
b) Yefsi Estiatorio
c) Figidini
d) Tel Aviv Waterfront
e) Sonia's Near East Market & Deli

Answer: b) Yefsi Estiatorio (This a fantastic Greek Restaurant is in the heart of Manhattan, NY)

91. Rhode Island's gorgeous landscape provide the perfect setting for all of these parks except?

a) Lincoln Woods State Park.
b) Goddard Memorial State Park
c) Colt State Park
d) Beavertail State Park
e) Hickory Run State Park
f) Snake Den State Park
g) Sabin Point Waterfront Park

Answer: e) Hickory Run State Park (This beautiful park is in Pennsylvania)

92. The Ocean state's coast are not the only scenes of picturesque water. Below are beautiful waterfalls in Rhode Island, except?

a) Paterson Fall, Paterson
b) Horseshoe Falls, Richmond
c) Pawtucket Falls, Pawtucket
d) Ponaganset Falls, Clayville
e) Manville Dam, Cumberland
f) Stepstone Falls Waterfall and Hiking Paths, West Greenwich

Answer: a) Paterson (The Paterson Falls are in New Jersey, but the remaining falls are all accessible to the visiting public in RI.)

93. Which of the following is not an outdoors kiddie playground in Rhode Island?

a) Brown Street Park Playground, Providence
b) Wickford Playground. North Kingstown
c) Fairfield Playground, East Greenwich
d) Fairfield Playground, Hope Valley
e) Kidz Kastle, Hope Valley

Answer: e) Kidz Kastle (This playground is indoors)

94. A fabulous burger can be had at all the following restaurants except?

a) Stanley's Famous Hamburgers, 535 Dexter St, Central Falls
b) Providence Burger Bar, 161 Douglas Ave, Providence
c) The Whiskey, 7563 W Sand Lake Rd, Orlando
d) Mission, 58 Aquidneck Ave #2, Middletown
e) Crazy Burger Cafe and Juice Bar, 144 Boon St, Narragansett
f) Chomp Kitchen and Drinks, 440 Child St, Warren

Answer: c) The Whiskey (This famous burger joint is in Orlando, FL, but the remaining on the list are delish!)

95. Which of the following vineyards are NOT in Rhode Island and open to the public for tasting?

a) WinterHawk Vineyards, 35 Yawgoo Pond Rd, West Kingston
b) Jalama Wines, 119 La Plaza, Palm Springs
c) Winery, Langworthy Rd, Westerly
d) Greenvale Vineyards, 582 Wapping Rd, Portsmouth
e) Newport Vineyards, 909 E Main Rd, Middletown
f) Leyden Farm Vineyard & Winery, 160 Plain Meeting House Rd, West Greenwich

Answer: b) Jalama Wines (It's in CA)

96. Rhode Island is known for its farms. Which of the listed organic farms is NOT in the Ocean State?

a) Wild Harmony Farm, 366 Victory Hwy C, Exeter
b) Windmist Farm, 71 Weeden Ln, Jamestown
c) Red Gate Farm, Aquinnah
d) Martinelli's Farm & Charcuterie, 56 Peep Toad Rd, North Scituate
e) White Rock Farm, 199 W Main Rd, Little Compton

Answer: c) Red Gate Farm (RGF is on Martha's Vineyard. All of the rest offer fresh meat, produce and poultry.)

97. Which of the following is an apple orchard open to the public?

a) Jaswell's Farm, 50 Swan Rd, Smithfield
b) Dame Farm and Orchards, 91B Brown Ave, Johnston
c) Rocky Brook Orchard, 997 Wapping Rd, Middletown
d) Appleland Orchard, 135 Smith Ave, Greenville
e) All of the above

Answer: e) All of the above (Pick your own and enjoy the day)

98. Which of the lighthouses below is NOT located in the Ocean State?

a) Newport Harbor Lighthouse
b) Blackwell Island Light
c) Block Island North Light
d) South East Lighthouse
e) Conimicut Lighthouse

Answer: b) Blackwell Island Light (This lighthouse is in New York)

99. Which of the following is NOT an amusement park in RI?

a) Bayview Fun Park
b) Sky Zone Trampoline Park
c) Yawgoo Valley Ski Area & Water Park
d) Great Adventures
e) Adventureland Family Fun Park

Answer: d) Great Adventures (This park is in New Jersey)

100. The Annual Newport Oyster & Chowder Festival is held when?

a) April
b) May
c) July
d) August

Answer: b) May (Held the 3rd weekend in May, The Bowen's Wharf Newport Oyster & Chowder Festival: Taste your way around Rhode Island – tickets sold daily.)

159

Photo Answers

Page 6: Point Judith Light built in 1857.

Page 22: See this round stone tower in Newport's Touro Park. The Newport Tower, also known as the Old Stone Mill, is what is left of a 17th century windmill.

Page 44: Cardines Field is the home of the Newport Gulls baseball team and is located at the corner of America's Cup Ave. and West Marlborough Street in Newport.

Page 58: Established in 1884, the US Naval War College – or the War College - provides advance professional study for naval officers.

Page 79: It is located at the Newport Casino, which opened as a social club in 1880, catering to Newport's summer elite.

Pages 81-90:

1. This is the First Baptist Church in America, located at 75 North Main Street in Providence.

2. This statue in Watch Hill portrays Ninigret, chief of the Niantic Indians.

3. Providence Riverwalk.

4. Groundswell Café and Bakery in Tiverton.

5. Bristol County Courthouse in Bristol.

6. This is Marble House in Newport, a Vanderbilt summer cottage.

7. Harkins Hall is the signature building on the campus of Providence College in Providence.

8. This is the Providence Library, located at 150 Empire Street.

9. This is the historic College Hill neighborhood of Providence.

10. This is the Customs building in Newport.

11. The Central Fire Station and the Post Office, both in Providence.

12. The Allendale Mill is an historic mill located in North Providence on the banks of the Woonasquatucket River.

13. Patience Island is located in Narragansett Bay.

14. This is an Indian monument in Exeter.

15. This post office is located in Block Island.

16. The St. Ann Arts and Cultural Center in Woonsocket is home t North America's largest collection of fresco paintings.

17. This is the Newport Bridge and Goat Island Lighthouse.

18. This gazebo is in Watch Hill in Westerly.

Page 110: The Vanderbilt Mansion, once owned by the business tycoor is now a luxury hotel.

Page 116: The house, located on Perry Street in Newport, is one of the best examples of shingle style architecture in the US.

Page 126: The Portuguese Discovery Monument in Newport pays tribute to Portuguese navigators of the Golden Age of exploration.